Who Do You Say That I Am

DR. JOSEPH MORRISON

ISBN 979-8-88685-601-9 (paperback)
ISBN 979-8-88685-602-6 (digital)

Christian Faith Publishing
832 Park Avenue
Meadville, PA 16335
www.christianfaithpublishing.com

All Scripture quotations, unless otherwise indicated, are taken from the King James Version.

Printed in the United States of America

CONTENTS

WOW (WORDS OF WISDOM) FROM THE HEART OF THE WRITER

I'm going to speak very directly and straight to the heart, because there is too much at stake to play games. When you know who God is, you will understand why He came.

As you read this book, it's my desire that it helps you have a hunger and thirst to know who God is. In the book of Matthew 5:6, it tells us, "Blessed are those who hungry and thirst for righteousness, for they shall be filled."

Even though the world is still under the curse of sin because of the fall of man (Adam and Eve), believers (Christians) can be freed from that curse and live the abundant life that belongs to them as a child of God when you know who He is.

> But those whose wish to boast should boast in this alone: that they truly know me and understand that I am the Lord who demonstrates unfailing love and who brings justice and righteous to the earth, and that I delight in these things. I, the Lord have spoken. (Jeremiah 9:24 NLT)

There is an old saying that goes like this: Give a man a fish; he will eat for a day. Teach a man how to fish, and he will eat for a lifetime.

Dr. Joseph says it like this: Give a man a word from God, and he will be inspired for a day. Teach a man to hear from God, and he will be inspired for a lifetime.

God has given us everything we need to live a victorious life (Ephesians 1:3). However, if you don't take the time to find out who Jesus is, what belongs to you as a child of God, and apply His principles to your life, you will not enjoy God's best for your life before you get to your finial destination.

A lot of people accept Jesus as their Savior and want God's best for their life, but they don't follow the principles that He have put in place for us to live by.

ACKNOWLEDGMENTS

I thank God for my wife, Mennie. She is one of my biggest supporters and one of my greatest encouragements. She has always wanted me to be the best man that I can be for the Lord, Jesus the Christ.

There is a saying that I used to hear that goes like this: Behind every good man, there is always a good woman. When I look back and see where the Lord has brought us from and how God has used her in my life to add the parts that I didn't have, I found those words to be a very true statement. I thank God for having so much mercy on me and allowing her to be part of His master plan for my life. It's like she jumped out of my dreams and into my reality of what a godly wife is according to the word of God.

Proverbs 31:10 (NLT) says it like this: Who can find a virtuous and capable wife? She is worth more than precious rubies. Her husband can trust her, and she will greatly enrich his life. She will not hinder him, but help him all her life.

I love her to life with all that's in me; however, falling in love with Jesus was the best thing I have ever done.

INTRODUCTION

I first give honor to my Lord and my Savior, my Healer, my Redeemer, my El Shaddai (the All-Sufficient One), the number one person in my life, Jesus the Christ. I thank Him for giving me this golden opportunity to write this my second book. Furthermore, I am humbled to share some of the wisdom that He has taught me over thirty-five years of my life since I accepted Him as my Savior and allowed Him to be my Lord.

Proverbs 4:7 tells us, "Wisdom is the principal thing; therefore get wisdom: and with all thy getting get understanding."

I am grateful to the Lord for inspiring me to write this book. The wisdom that is written on these pages comes from being influenced by decades of experiences that have helped mold me into the man of God that I am today.

We face challenges in our society today that don't have simple solutions. We live in an increasingly frustrated world. A world with more senseless violence, polarized political debates, and racial inequality.

After the first twenty-five years of my life trying to make it without God, I was at a point where I couldn't even think of anything to try that might work. I knew about God because my mother raised her kids up in the church, but I didn't know who He was for me. I only knew what I heard preached about the man named Jesus.

Although it was a traditional church, I thank God that the seed of the man named Jesus was planted in my heart. Although I knew what I heard about Jesus, until I got to know Him for myself, I didn't know who He really was.

God wants everyone to know who He really is. He wants to put His super with our natural, that we may live a supernatural life. Not just talk about the life that He died for us to have on earth, but to enjoy it until we get to our final destination. John 10:10 tells us that He came that we might have life and have it more abundantly.

You have to understand as a Christian (a child of God) that our victory has been secured. While you and I are still on earth, we need to live in the light of the truth of the victory gained through the finished work of the cross by Jesus Christ.

Although our victory has been secured by Jesus, we are still in a battle (a spiritual battle). Second letter to the Corinthians 10: 3–5 tells us,

> For though we walk in the flesh, we do not war after the flesh: For the weapons of our warfare are not carnal, but mighty through God to the pulling down of strong holds; Casting down imaginations, and every high thing that exalteth itself against the knowledge of God, and bringing into captivity every thought to the obedience of Christ.

If Satan (the devil, our enemy) can keep you from taking the spiritual realm seriously as a Christian, he knows that he can keep you away from where your victory is found. If he (Satan, our enemy) can distract you with people or things you can see, taste, touch, hear, or smell, he knows that he can keep you from living a life of victory that is yours as a child of God.

You as a child of God have to understand that we are in a war that our eyes can't see. We are in a spiritual war, and if the devil (our enemy) can keep you from taking this spiritual realm seriously, you will not live in the victory that belongs to you before you get to heaven. You will go to heaven when this life is over, but you will not enjoy the trip or live in victory before you get there.

Because of the resurrection of Jesus Christ, the devil (Satan, our enemy) no longer has authority over you to defeat you. His only means to overcome you is to deceive you. To try and make you think and believe that the battle has not been won.

I pray that as you read this book, it will be a blessing to your life as you learn what God's Word has to say about who He is and the covenant that He has established for His people.

I learned coming up in the school of hard knocks that there is an easy way and a hard way of doing everything. When I learned God's way of doing things according to His word, and when I started to apply His principles to my everyday walk of life, my life has never been the same, and my life has been blessed without measure.

When you apply God's principles in your life (I call it working the Word), your life will never be the same. You must understand this. You can be a born-again Christian on your way to heaven, but if you don't work the Word of God (the Bible) in your life, the Word will not work. The promises of God will not be fulfilled in your life until you get to your finial destination. I know that is tight, but believe me, it's right.

Although my life has been blessed without measure, after I learned God's way of doing things and applying them to my life, there have still been challenges that I have faced and had to overcome.

However, thanks be to God who always gives us the victory.

True Christianity is not the absence of tests and trails, but the strength and comfort of Jesus through the Holy Spirit that will bring us victoriously through to the other side.

God tells us in the book of John 16:33, "In the world ye shall have tribulation [tests and trials]: but be of good cheer; I have overcome the world."

The words that God has allowed me to write on the pages of this book are not from my education, but they come from my revelation that God has given me over the years as I took Him at His word. I truly believe that education is good and education is knowledge.

I also believe, based on my experiences, that education without revelation is a misrepresentation.

Furthermore, I say that because if the promises of God have not become a reality or fulfilled in your life, they are just words on a piece of paper. However, when God has performed His promises in your life according to His word, nobody can tell you that His promises in Him are not "yes" and "amen" (2 Corinthians 1:20).

You must understand that accepting Jesus as your Savior is the best decision that you will ever make in this life. However, God is not just the starting point of your life; He has to be the source of your life if you want His results.

Accepting Jesus as your Savior is the best decision you can make in this life because your salvation will be sealed from that day forward until eternity. Although your salvation is sealed, it only prepares you for heaven. It's how you live your life before you get there.

In this life until we get to our final destination, we can't put Jesus around our lives. Our lives have to be surrounded by Jesus in order to get the results that He laid His life down for us to have.

> Jesus saith unto him, I am the way the truth
> and the life: no man cometh unto the father but
> by me. (John 14:6)

To discover your purpose in this life, you must turn to God's Word (the Holy Bible). You must build your life on eternal truths that only comes from the Word of God. It is in Christ that we find out who we are and what belongs to us as a child of God.

Those who build their lives on God's teaching or the Word of God will have security and stability. Those who reject God's teachings and try to do it the world's way will not stand the pressure of this life. You will get the world's result, which are doom, gloom, and defeat.

In this life that we are in until we get to our final destination, there will be many challenges that we will face, whether you have accepted Jesus as your Savior or not.

> I have told you all this so that you may have
> peace in me. Here on earth, you will have many
> trials and sorrows. But take heart, because I have
> overcome the world. (John 16:33 NLT)

WOW (words of wisdom): The more there is left to chance, the less chance there is for you to walk in victory and in the abundant life that belongs to you as a Christian, a child of the living God.

A lot of people want to give Jesus their heart, but they stop short of giving Him their lives. Jesus not only wants to be your Savior, He wants to be your Lord. If He's Lord of your life, He wants to have something to say about how you live, what you say, what you do, and who you fellowship with.

God can't just be the starting point of your life. You have to allow Him to be your Lord and the source of your life.

The Question

As so much is happening in our country and around the world, I believe God is asking every Christian this question today: Who do you say that I am?

Because it's hard to understand the depths of what Jesus did on the cross for us, many people (even many Christians) fail to live up to the privileges that are theirs as a child of God.

We are living in a generation with diseases that no man can cure, and with problems no man can solve. These are hard, challenging times for many Americans and those that are living around the world.

Second letter to Timothy 3:1 NLT tells us, "You should know this, Timothy, that in the last days there will be very difficult times [perilous times]."

The Bible tells us that in the last days, perilous times (hard times) will come. In addition to the different viruses and other diseases, dangerous storms, wars, civil unrest, etc., I believe that you can agree with me that we are living in perilous times.

Although we are troubled on every side, you have to know for yourself as a child of the living God the answer to that question. You cannot go on who God is to another person; you have to know that answer for yourself. You have to know and believe that hard times don't change God. He tells us in Malachi 3:6 NLT, "I am the Lord, and I do not change. That is why you descendants of Jacob are not already completely destroyed."

As this book is being written, it had come to a point just in the United States alone, in March 2022, that there were over one million (1,000,000) people that have died from the COVID-19 pandemic and gone out into eternity.

For generations to come, if the Lord tarries, they will be reading in the history books about what happened in this historical event that took place in our generation.

In January 2021 in California, it reported that at one point in that month, a person was dying and going out into eternity every fifteen seconds. Hospitals were full and not accepting any more patients because there were no more rooms available.

Of all the people that have gone out into eternity, as a believer in God, our hearts should have been heavy for those that have lost loved ones. However, our hearts should have also been heavy for the ones that died and didn't know Jesus as their Savior.

Everybody knows that one day we are all going to pass from this life and go out into eternity. I will tell you like an older preacher used to tell me before he died. He would tell me not to believe him but to believe the Word of God. The Word of God tells us in Hebrews 9:27, "And it is appointed unto man once to die, but after this the judgment."

We are living in a season, as this book is being written, that because of the pandemic, if you had to be admitted to the hospital, you will be alone. No one could come and visit you, not even your family (father, mother, or your children). They were not even allowing hospital chaplains or pastors to come and visit people because of the pandemic.

We are living in some hard times, and I believe that this is a question that we need to all ask and know ourselves about God. Who do you say that He is in your life?

Even when Jesus walked the earth, hard times came, and some people stopped believing and trusting in Him. He even turned to His disciples and asked them, Are you going to forsake me too? (John 6:67).

WOW (words of wisdom): So many today want to be associated with Jesus, but not everyone wants to commit to Him and His ways.

Second Timothy 4:3 tells us, "For the time will come when they will not endure sound doctrine; but after their own lusts shall they heap to themselves teachers, having itching ears."

With so much going on in the world today that can't be explained, there are many Christians that are turning away from the foundation that was established by God.

Even though the world is still under the curse of sin because of the fall of man (Adam and Eve), believers can be freed from that curse and live the abundant life that belongs to them as a child of God, even in the midst of what's going on in the world.

- Now I said believers can be freed, because you can be a believer and not believe.
- You can be saved and not be a Christian (Christlike).
- You can be saved on your way to heaven and not stand in God's righteousness with authority.

As you read this book, my desire is that it helps you to see this walk of life like it really is as a born-again child of the living God.

I don't write words to make you feel good. I deliver messages from the Lord to try and teach you how to do good so that you can receive everything that Jesus laid His life down for you to have here on earth before you get to your finial destination.

Second letter to the Corinthians 5:17 says, "Therefore if any man be in Christ, he is a new creature; old things are passed away; behold, all things are become new."

God makes it clear in the book of 1 Corinthians 2:14–15: "But the natural man receiveth not the things of the spirit of God, for they are foolish unto him, neither can he know them because they are spiritually discerned. but he that is spiritual judgeth all things, yet he himself is judge of no man."

As a Christian, a child of the living God, we have God's unlimited power available to us to change our lives once we commit to Him and take responsibility for our actions.

Like I said, so many today want to be associated with Jesus, but not everyone wants to commit to Him and His ways.

Once you realize that Jesus is the only reason that we are living, moving and have our beings, you will look to Him to direct your steps. In the book of John 15: 5, Jesus tells us, "I am the vine, ye are the branches: He that abideth in me, and I in him, the same bringeth forth much fruit: for without me ye can do nothing."

Will you ever be perfect? No. Will you always make mistakes? Yes, all of your life. Until your spirit (the real you) gets out of your temporary dwelling place. This piece of flesh that our spirit is living in, you will always miss the mark.

If we could have hit the mark or knew how to make it without a Savior, Jesus would not have had to come in the form of a man and die for you and for me.

Circumstances and traditions may have robbed you in your past. You don't have to let your circumstances rob you of your future. Once you know and understand who Jesus is and what belongs to you as a child of God, your life will never be the same, and you will understand why He came.

Once you understand and realize that you have the greater one living on the inside of you, the old excuses that you use to have to justify your lifestyle don't hold up anymore. First letter to John 4:4 tells us, "You are of God little children, and have overcome them, because greater is he that is in you than he that is in the world."

The Holy Spirit, who was on the outside of us, convicting us of our sins, now lives on the inside of us when we opened our heart and accepted Jesus as our Savior. "Behold, I stand at the door and knock; if any man hear my voice and open the door, I will come in to him, and will sup with him and he with me" (Revelation 3:20).

Once you understand that, and your eyes are open to the truth from the word of God, you will truly understand why He came and the price that Jesus paid for your soul.

Although we have accepted Jesus as our Savior, and we are now a child of God, we still have a choice to make if we want to follow His will and His ways for our life. Until you make the conscious decision to follow Him, you will not be able to answer the question with confidence of who He is.

We have a choice of who we are going to serve in this life. God tells us in the book of Joshua 24:15: "And if it seems evil unto you to serve the Lord, choose you this day whom you will serve. But as for me and my house, we will serve the Lord."

CHAPTER 2

The Sovereignty of God

One songwriter wrote a song, and one of the lines in the lyrics goes like this: "He's real, real, Jesus is real to me / and He gave me perfect liberty / so many people doubt Him / but I can't live without Him / That is why I love Him so because He's so real to me."

Do you know for yourself that God is good? Do you know for yourself that God is faithful? You can ask people about God, and they will tell you that God is good all the time and all the time God is good.

I have learned that as a Christian, the world system wants us to believe that the Word of God doesn't work. That God doesn't love you. That God is not real.

If you are a Christian, God has given us everything we need to live a victorious life while we are here on earth. If you don't, it's nobody's fault but your own.

I know so many Christians that are saved on their way to heaven, but they are not enjoying the trip. I know well what Hosea 4:6 means when God tells us that His people (Christians) are destroyed for a lack of knowledge.

Let me give you an example. If you had a million dollars deposited into your account and you didn't know it was there, it wouldn't do you any good, right?

As it is in the natural, so it is in the Spirit. You can be saved on your way to heaven, but if you don't take the time to find out the price that has been paid for you and what has been deposited in you, it will not do you any good. If you don't take the time to find out what has been made available to you and what belongs to you as a child of God, it will not do you any good before you get to heaven.

God told me over thirty-five years ago that somebody needs to demonstrate this walk of life. I have willingly positioned myself to receive what God tells us in His word that we can have while we are here on earth.

Isaiah 1:19 tells us, "If you are willing and obedient, you shall eat the good of the land."

Am I perfect? No. Do I make mistakes? Yes. Ecclesiastes 7:20 tells us, "There is not a righteous man on earth that does everything right and never sin."

Romans 3:23 tells us, "For all have sin and come short of the glory of God."

But when you learn who you are in Christ, not who He is in you but who you are in Him, you will understand grace. You see, if you don't understand grace, you will have a performance relationship with God.

It's a lot that I don't know, and it's a lot of places that I might not ever go, but it's one thing that I do know—that God is real, and He's real in my soul.

I don't understand it all, but I believe it all.

I am going to teach on a subject that has a lot of controversy in the body of Christ.

John 8:32 tells us, "You shall know the truth and the truth shall make you free." God told me to always tell you the truth so that you can accept it or reject it. If I don't tell you the truth, I am rejecting it for you.

WOW (words of wisdom): Not everything that we face can be changed, but nothing can be changed until it is faced.

It's a lot of problems that we will experience; tests, trials, and hardships will come to all of us in this life. In John 16:33, Jesus tells us, "These things I have spoken unto you, that in Him, we will have peace; in the world we shall have tribulations (tests and trails) but be of good cheer, He has overcome the world."

The Word of God tells us in Matthew 5:45 NKJV, "For He makes His sun rise on the evil and on the good, and sends rain on the just and on the unjust."

There are so many that have yet to understand that we are living in a fallen world. When Adam and Eve sinned in the garden of Eden, that opened the door for all the things that we are experiencing in our world today.

When Adam and Eve sinned, the world was cursed. The world is still under a curse, and it will be under a curse until Jesus comes back.

Yes, there are a lot of situations that come with this life, and there are hardships that can come with this life, but I hear many ministers of the gospel telling the people of God that God allows bad thing to happen to them.

Being raised in a traditional church and listening to that kind of teaching coming up made me not want to be a Christian. It seems like everything you did as a Christian would send you to hell.

Instead of teaching faith, many pastors taught fear. Instead of teaching the goodness and mercy of God, many taught that God would allow bad things to happen to you to teach you a lesson or to stop you from during wrong.

Most Christians say that they believe that God is good, but they don't live like it. Most say that God loves them, but they don't think they are good enough for God to do anything good for them, or they don't think they are good enough for them to be healed.

The answer to that is this: None of us are good enough for God to do anything good for us. We all deserve to go to hell, but because of who God is, we don't get what we deserve.

Because of the covenant (a formal binding agreement) that God has established for them that accept Him as their Savior, we don't get what we deserve because He is bound by His word.

Lamentation 3:22–23 say it like this: "It is the Lord's mercies that we are not consumed; because His compassion fail not; they are new to us every morning; great is thou faithfulness."

I thank God for His grace and mercy. Grace is giving us what we don't deserve, and mercy is keeping from us what we do deserve.

God's grace and mercy are new to us every morning. If you don't understand grace, you will have a performance relationship with God. Yes, we want to live a life that is pleasing to God that will bring Him glory, but you should never depend on your performance to make you think that you are in right standing with God.

People ask me all the time, "Why are things not working for me?" I believe the number one reason the word of God is not working in a person's life is because of deception.

I want to try to help you to have assurance that God is faithful and that God will look over His word to perform it.

The Lord had me write the teaching in this chapter over fifteen years ago. This message is not a new message, but it's a now message. There are so many today that don't have a biblical world view, and God is getting blamed for a lot of things that He doesn't have anything to do with.

I'm going to teach what I think is the biggest deception in the body of Christ. I'm going to teach on a subject that has a lot of controversy in the body of Christ. The sovereignty of God.

I hear so many pastors and preachers preach that God controls everything. That God supernaturally controls everything that happens, and nothing can happen unless God associates it or gives the devil permission to do it.

Now if you are one of those that believe that, I'm going to the Word of God to show you that that's not in the Word of God. I'm going to show you that that's a religious traditional spirit and the doctrine of man.

If you as a Christians believe that God controls everything, then you are attributing all the terrible things that are happening to God. It makes God responsible for them—all the murders, rapes, and all the bad things that are happening around the world.

If you believe that God didn't do it but He gave the devil permission to do it, then that makes God responsible for them. If that is what you think and believe, it is hard to believe that God is a good God, because it's a lot of bad things going on around us and in the world.

I understand that if you have not grown up in the things of God, you are still a baby Christian, and you may be one of those Christians that blame God for what the devil is doing in your life. Why do I say that? Because you have not transformed your mind by the Word of God yet.

You must understand that God doesn't deal with us in the flesh. We have to deal with our flesh and bring it under subjection to our spirit. God deals with us in the spirit. In the book of John 4:24, it tells us, "God is a Spirit: and they that worship Him must worship Him in spirit and in truth."

I know that some of you right now are saying, and I hear this all the time, "Well, God is sovereign. I do believe that God is sovereign if you use it correctly. Not only that, but I do believe that God is the head of everything. Furthermore, I do believe that God is all-powerful.

Let's look at what the dictionary says about the word sovereign. If you use it as a noun, the word sovereign means chief of state and monarchy, or a form of a British corn that's worth one pound.

When you use the word sovereign as an adjective, it's talking about paramount or supreme. I do believe that God is supreme; I do believe that He is the top of everything. I do believe that no one gives God orders or makes Him do anything.

Sovereign also means having supreme rank or power. I believe that God is supreme. That He is almighty. I do believe that God is highest in rank, order, and authority.

Let me tell you what happens and why so many believe the way they do. One of the translations of the Bible, which is one of the most popular translations, took the words *Almighty God* that was in the King James and substituted it with *sovereign Lord* over three thousand times in that translation.

That's the translation that popularizes the term sovereign. It didn't exist until this translation came out. They substituted *sovereign Lord* for *Lord God almighty*.

I'm not against the word sovereign if it is used correctly. Other definitions include excellence, having rank or power, independent—like a sovereign state. The United States is sovereign. On July 4,

1776, it broke away from Great Britain and is now independent and is a self-determined country.

Another definition of sovereign is excellence that comes from a Latin word that means super, above. I believe that God is super, that God is above, that God is highest in rank, order, and that God is supreme, and I believe that God is excellent. If you want to use the word sovereign the way the dictionary talks about it, God is sovereign.

But if you use the word sovereign and believe the way religion talks about it, I reject it, and that's not the truth about God. Sovereign, the way some religions describe it, says that God sovereignly controls everything. That nothing happens unless He has His hand in it. He either initiates it or the devil has to go to Him and get permission from Him to do it.

That's not what the word of God teaches, and if you believe that, I don't see how you can have a good image of God.

> In whom the god of this world hath blinded
> the minds of them which believe not, lest the
> light of the glorious gospel of Christ; who is
> the image of God, should shine unto them.
> (2 Corinthians 4:4)

Let me put it this way. If you thought that I had something to do with every problem that happens in your family or in your life, you wouldn't like me. I could have stopped it, but I didn't because I thought you deserved it, or I wanted to teach you something. I didn't do it, but I gave permission for it to happen. I can guarantee that you wouldn't like me.

Or let me put it this way. If some men broke in your house and put a gun to your husband's head, tied him up, and made him watch them take turns raping his wife and daughter, you can say that God didn't do it but He allowed it to happen. What kind of sense does that make?

If you think that we serve a God like that, how can you have a good image of God? The one that created you, the one that took our place on the cross to get back everything that was lost, that we could have a right to the tree of life.

If you believe that about God, you are being deceived, and that's not the God of the Bible. The word of God tells us in the book of John 15:13, "Greater love hast no man than this; that a man lay down his life for a friend."

There is not a nation in the world that would let me live if they thought I was the one who caused or allowed all the deaths and the bad things that are going on in the world.

But this is the presentation of God by so many today—that God controls everything. God is not the author of the ungodly things that's going on in the world and the things that come against us. If you believe that as being truth about God, the Word of God will have no effect in your life as a child of God (Matthew 15:6).

You will still go to heaven when this life is over if you have accepted Jesus as your Savior, but you will not enjoy the trip before you get there.

WOW (words of wisdom): if you ever suspect or think that God is the source of your misfortunes, hardships, or sickness, you will never be able to have enough faith to believe Him for deliverance from them.

It always gets me when I go to a funeral after someone passes and I talk to people and they say things like "God is too wise to make a mistake" or "we know that God had a plan."

What they are saying is that a person's number must have been up, as if God's got a date circled on the calendar that says that your day and your number is up.

I hear people say things like "Well, you know, God only gave us threescore and ten. For those of you that may not understand the King James, that's seventy years, and you could live eighty years if you are strong.

This number (seventy) has often been mistaken as a set span of life for all mankind. It was not intended to refer to anyone except those Israelites under the curse during that particular forty years. Seventy years has never been the average span of life for humanity. Our covenant years are 120 years.

It tells us in the Book of Genesis 6:3, "And the LORD said, 'My spirit shall not always strive with man, for that he also is flesh: yet his days shall be an hundred and twenty years.'"

In Genesis 47:9, when Jacob, the father of the twelve tribes, had reached 130 years, he complained that he had not attained to the years of his ancestors. Moses lived to be 120 years old. Aaron lived 123 years. Miriam was several years older, and Joshua 110 years of age.

Our covenant years are 120 years. Seventy is not the max; it's a minimal that God gave everyone.

Some people die prematurely before their covenant years. If you go out and become an alcoholic and destroy your liver, you are going to die. If you smoke drugs or shoot drugs in your veins, it's a chance you will have heart failure, and you may die. If you smoke tobacco, and it causes cancer in your body, you can speed up the process, and you could die a premature death.

But that's not always the case; you can be doing everything right but have not transformed your mind by the Word of God and know God's promises of protection for you, so premature death can still happen.

You can be born again, on your way to heaven, but if you don't know God's promises concerning every area of your life, those promises will not be manifested. The Word of God gives us promises of protection, provision, health, and so much more.

You can be born again, on your way to heaven, but if you don't know who you are in Christ and what God has promised for you in this life, you will not have any hope or confidence.

First letter to the Corinthians 15:19 tells us, "If in this life only we have hope in Christ, we are of all men most miserable."

I thank God that I'm saved, and if I don't wake up in the morning, everything will be all right. But if you only have hope in Christ for salvation and not for what He died for you to have in this life, you will be of all men most miserable. If you believe that God allows everything bad that happens to you, how can you have a good image of God?

Like I said, if you ever suspect or think that God is the source of your misfortunes, hardships, or sickness, you will never be able to have enough faith to believe Him for deliverance from them.

If you believe that God is the source of your hardships, how can you believe Revelation 1:18 that tells us, "God went to hell, and He took from the devil the keys of death hell and the grave"?

How can you believe John 10:10—that God came so that we can have life and have it more abundantly?

How can you believe 3 John 2: "Beloved, I wish above all things that thou prosper and be in health, even as thou soul prospereth."

If you believe that God is sovereign and He allows everything that happens, how can you believe Romans 8:31–32 where it says, "What shall we say to these things? If God be for us, who can be against us? He that spared not His own son, but delivered him up for us all, how shall He not with Him also freely give us all things?"

In order to receive all the benefits God desires to give you, you must be absolutely sure that He is a good God. You must be certain that His will for you is health, not sickness; prosperity, not poverty; happiness, not sorrow.

We live in a fallen world, and God told Adam and Eve that "if you eat of this tree, you're going to die." God didn't start death; man started death.

We are the ones that brought corruption in the world. The world is a deadly place, and it amazes me that some religions says that it was God's will. If you think that God is the one that is allowing or have a purpose for you being sick, why go to the doctor?

If you believe God didn't do it but He allowed the devil to cause sickness to come against you, why ask for prayer? Why don't you let it take its course? If you say God didn't do it but He allowed it, why don't you let it take its course and not go against the will of God?

If you believe that, then that's not the God of the Bible, because that is not what the Bible teaches. That's not the person who created you. But let me submit this to you. There are a lot of Christians that have been taught a certain way, and they are not going to let anything stand in the way of what they believe, not even the Bible.

God has a perfect plan for each one of us, but we have to cooperate. We have to take some responsibility for how we live our life and what's going on in our life. We have to take our rightful place and learn how to release the power of God that has been made available to us to use until we get to our final destination.

> You are of God little children and have overcome them because greater is He that is in you than he that is in the world. (1 John 4:4)

> You shall receive power after the Holy Ghost have come upon you. (Acts 1:8)

> I give you power and authority over all devils and to cure all diseases. (Luke 9:1)

> I give you power to tread on serpents and scorpions; and over all the power of the devil, and nothing shall by any means hurt you. (Luke 10:19)

> Verily, I say unto you, whatsoever you bind on earth shall be bound in heaven and whatsoever you loose on earth shall be loose in heaven. (Matthew 18:18)

WOW (words of wisdom): God will allow what you will allow. Victory already belongs to us as a child of God, but what level of victory we walk in here on earth is up to us. God has done everything He is going to do. He let them hang Him high and swing Him wide, and the last two things He said were "Forgive them, Lord, for they know not what they do." Then He said, "It is finished," and He passed the baton to us to finish this race to the finish line.

> Wherefore my beloved, as you have always obeyed, not as in my present only, but now much

> more in my absence, work out your own salva-
> tions with fear and trembling [respect and obedi-
> ence]. (Philippians 2:12)

We are the ones who limit God. Religion has come alone with theology and says that everything that happens in your life is God's will because God is sovereign.

God's sovereignty knows everything. He knows the end from the beginning, but He has given us the keys to the kingdom to walk in victory.

So many believers have not taken their rightful place in the kingdom of God. They don't know who they are in Christ and what belongs to them as a child of God, so they just kick back and say what's going to be will be.

Let me ask you a question. If you believe that what's going to be will be, why be obedient to the things of God? If you believe that what's going to be will be, why serve God?

WOW (words of wisdom): If you believe that God controls everything, how can He hold you accountable for the wrongs you do and everything that happens to you?

Let me show you some scriptures.

> How oft did they provoke him in the wil-
> derness, and grieve him in the desert! Yea, they
> turned back and tempted God, and limited the
> Holy One of Israel. They remembered not his
> hand, nor the day when he delivered them from
> the enemy. (Psalm 78:40–42)

> See then that you walk circumspectly [care-
> ful] not as fools but as wise. Redeeming the
> time because the days are evil. Wherefore be not
> unwise but understanding what the will of the
> Lord is. (Ephesians 5:15–17)

God is not a man, that He does not lie. He is not a human, that He should change his mind. Has He ever spoken and fail to act? Has He ever promised and not carried it through? (Numbers 23:19 NLT)

The Lord is not slack concerning His promises, as some men count slackness. (2 Peter 3:9)

For you know the grace of our Lord Jesus Christ that though he was rich, yet for your sake he became poor, that though his poverty might be rich. (2 Corinthians 8:9)

Blessed be the God and father of our Lord Jesus Christ, who hath blessed us with all spiritual blessings in heavenly places in Christ. (Ephesians 1:3)

I will worship toward thy holy temple, and praise thy name for thy loving kindness and for thy truth: for thou hast magnified (put) thy word above all thy name. (Psalm 138:2)

Remember them that are in bonds, as bound with them; and them which suffer adversity, as being yourselves also in the body. (Hebrews 1:3)

Christ has redeemed us from the curse of the law, being made a curse for us; for it is written, curse is every one that hangeth on a tree. (Galatians 3:13)

Submit yourselves therefore to God. Resist the devil, and he will flee from you. (James 4:7)

> Herein is our love made perfect, that we may
> have boldness in the Day of Judgment: because as
> He is, so are we in this world. (1 John 4:17)

God has a perfect plan for each one of us, but we have to cooperate. We have to take some responsibility for this walk of life.

If you are one of those Christians that just sit back and believe what's going to be will be, that God is Sovereign and everything that happens to you He gave the devil permission to do it, the devil will come in your house, sit at your table, eat your lunch, and pop the bag in your face.

We have to take some responsibility. We have to take our rightful place and learn how to release the power of God. This power has already been made available to us to use against our enemy (the devil) that we can live in victory until we get to our final destination.

You might be asking, How do I cooperate and take my rightful place? I'm glad you asked that question. There are several things you must do.

The first, and the most important thing, is to accept Jesus as your Savior, because none of this will work for you if you are not connected to the power source. Then you have to learn what belongs to you and who you are as a child of God.

Second letter to Timothy 2:15 tells us, "Study to show thyself approve unto God; a workman that needeth not to be ashamed, rightly dividing the word of truth."

Second letter to Timothy 2:26 tells us, "And that they may recover themselves out of the snares of the devil who are taking captive by him at his will."

This is one of the reasons why God gave us His word.

> My son, attend [take charge of, look after]
> to my words; incline thine ear unto my sayings.
> Let them not depart from thine eyes; keep them
> in the midst of thine heart. For they are life unto
> them that find them and health to all their flesh.
> (Proverbs 4:20)

Once you learn who you are in Christ and the power that has been made available to you to use, then you have to do what I call the four *R*s.

You have to *recognize, repent, renounce,* and *resist.* This is not something that you can do just once. This has to be a lifestyle if you want to live a victorious life and enjoy the abundant life that belongs to you as a child of God.

- You have to *recognize* when things are coming against you and when you are not walking in obedience according to the word of God.
- You have to *repent* to God when you have done something that is contrary to His word because that will open the door for the devil.
- You have to *renounce* the demonic spirit that is trying to deceive you by releasing the power of God that is made available to you to use in the time of need.
- You have to *resist* the devil, and he will flee from you.

You must understand that this principle is not something you can do just once. It has to be a lifetime commitment. You can never go on vacation when it comes to spiritual warfare.

God is not your enemy, God is your friend. God wants us to have the best that this world has to offer. Psalm 24:1 tells us, "The earth is the Lord's and the fullness thereof; the world and they that dwell therein."

> Teach those who are rich in this world not to
> be proud and not to trust in their money, which
> is so unreliable. Their trust should be in God,
> who richly gives us all we need for our enjoy-
> ment. (1 Timothy 6:17 NLT)

If you want to keep living the way you are living and believe that God's sovereignly controls everything that happens to you, I'm not mad at you. God is not mad at you. But you can never say from this day, after reading this chapter, that you didn't know the truth.

If you are one of those Christians that don't know how the devil operates, you will be one of those Christians that blame God for what the devil is doing in your life.

God is sovereign if you use it correctly. But if you use the word sovereign the way religion talks about it, I reject it, and that's not the truth about the God we serve, and that's not the God of the Bible.

WOW (words of wisdom): If you ever suspect or think that God is the source of your misfortunes or sickness, you will never be able to have enough faith to believe Him for deliverance from them.

CHAPTER 3

Don't Protest the Process

I am convinced after the election in 2020 that the vast numbers of people that confess Jesus as their Savior in the United States don't have a biblical world view.

I know that many do not believe that the things that are going on in this country and around the world are contrary to the Word of God. Because there are many that are against God's plan for life.

> You made all the delicate, inner parts of my body and knit me together in my mother's womb. (Psalm 139:13 NLT)

> Before I formed thee in the belly I knew thee. (Jeremiah 1:5)

God makes it clear in the book of John 10:10 that He came so that we can have life and have it more abundantly. He came to give life and not take it.

This is not something that has just started. We are living in a time when this country has planted so many bad seeds. Just as a farmer that plants seeds start to grow, the word of God, which is the seed of God (Luke 8:11), starts to deepen and grow within a person as they continue to seek God and study His word. The same is true with a nation. Unfortunately, the United States has planted a lot of bad seeds.

Galatians 6:7 tells us, "Be not deceived, God is not mocked; for whatever a man soweth, that shall he will also reap." "You reap what you sow" is a proverb that says future consequences are inevitably shaped by present actions.

Dr. Joseph's version says it this way: Yesterday's choices (seeds planted) are today's reality, and today's choices (seeds planted) are going to be tomorrow's results.

There is a spiritual law that is in place that affects everyone regardless if they follow Jesus or not. It's called sowing and reaping.

Genesis 8:22 tells us, "While the earth remaineth, seedtime and harvest, and cold and heat, and summer and winter, and day and night shall not cease."

Whatever we do each day, good or bad, is sowing seeds, and we will reap a harvest from the seeds that we have sown whether we want it or not.

God designed this world with a sense of order. It was designed out of a heart of great love for us. If we choose to go against the Word of God, we will reap corruption in this life.

God has given us free will to make our choices, but there are consequences for the choices that we make. We must be mindful of how we conduct ourselves and our daily affairs.

Although we live under a better covenant that God has prepared for us by His grace, God has put laws in place, and you can't get around them no matter how hard you try.

You can be saved and still reap corruption. You can be saved on your way to heaven and not enjoy the trip. Why? Because you have not aligned yourself to God's master plan for your life. When you are not following the master plan that God has put in place for His people (Christians), you are not getting the best out of your investment.

Like I said, everybody wants to be associated with Jesus, but not everyone wants to commit to Him and His way of doing things.

If you are reaping corruption in your life, you are following the world system (which is fleshly) and not God's system (which is spiritual), and these two are against each other.

Don't believe me, believe the word.

> For the flesh lusteth the Spirit, and the Spirit against the flesh; and these are contrary the one to the other, so that you cannot do the things that you would. (Galatians 5:17)

I don't believe Christians have problems anymore. I believe that Christians have opportunities. Opportunities to prove that the Word of God is true. You should not protest the process if you want the best for your life as a Christian. There is a process that each one of us must go through to understand who Jesus really is, and we should not protest the process.

Yes, there is a cross that everyone has to bear in this life. It tells us in the book of Matthew 16:24, "Then said Jesus unto his disciples, 'If any man will come after me, let him deny himself, and take up his cross, and follow me.'"

Just as Jesus bore His cross for us, every person has their own cross to bear. What's on your cross is not on my cross, and what's on my cross is not on the next person's cross. Everyone has their own cross to bear, but there is good news.

Although everyone has their own cross to bear in this life, no matter what's on your cross, the principles of God for deliverance are the same. When you learn what God has promised concerning that area of your life, and when you practice the principles (work the Word) that He has put in place, He promises that He would deliver you.

Psalm 34:19 tells us, "Many are the afflictions of the righteous: but the LORD delivereth him out of them all."

When you get to know who Jesus is, you will understand why He came. Once you understand why He came, and develop a personal relationship with Him, your life will never be the same, and your faith will begin to grow.

WOW (words of wisdom): What you do in this life makes a difference. You are the one who has to decide what kind of difference you want to make. And you should not protest the process.

In the book of Matthew 16: 13–20, the NLT translation says it like this:

> When Jesus came to the region of Caesarea Philippi, he asked his disciples, "Who do people say that the Son of Man is?"
>
> "Well," they replied, "some says John the Baptist, some say Elijah, and others say Jeremiah or one of the other prophets."
>
> Then he asked them, "But who do you say I am?"
>
> Simon Peter answered, "You are the Messiah, the Son of the living God."
>
> Jesus replied, "You are blessed, Simon son of John, because my Father in heaven has revealed this to you. You did not learn this from any human being.
>
> Now I say to you that you are Peter (which means 'rock'), and upon this rock I will build my church, and all the powers of hell will not conquer it.
>
> And I will give you the keys of the Kingdom of Heaven. Whatever you forbid on earth will be forbidden in heaven, and whatever you permit on earth will be permitted in heaven."
>
> Then he sternly warned the disciples not to tell anyone that he was the Messiah.

With all that is going on in our world today, I want to encourage you by letting you know that no matter what's going on around us, the same God that has protected, provided, and made provisions for us thus far is the same God today. When we allow Jesus to be Lord over our life and to be our refuge, we can have courage in knowing that He is always with us.

Hebrews 13: 5 tells us, "For he hast said, I will never leave thee nor forsake thee."

Hebrews 13: 8 tells us, "Jesus Christ the same yesterday, today and forever."

Philippians 4:19 tells us, "But my God shall supply all your needs according to His riches in glory by Christ Jesus."

Isaiah 54:17 tells us, "No weapon that is formed against thee shall prosper; and every tongue that rise against thee in judgment thou shall condemn."

Psalm 91:10 tells us, "There shall no evil shall befall thee, neither shall any plague come nigh thy dwelling.

"No evil will conquer you; no plague will come near your home" (NLT).

Exodus 23:25 tells us, "And you shall serve the Lord your God, and He shall bless thy bread, and thy water; and I will take sickness away from the mist of thee."

COVID-19, influenza, cancer, pneumonia, and flu, whatever the case may be, it shall not come near our dwelling because we have been redeemed from the curse.

Galatians 3:13 tells us, "Christ hath redeemed us from the curse of the law, being made a curse for us: for it is written, cursed is everyone that hangeth on a tree."

God tells us in Matthew 5:45, "For He maketh His sun to rise on the evil and on the good, and sendeth rain on the just and on the unjust." Although as Christians, children of the living God, who are saved and on our way to heaven, we can't deny our natural existence and what's going on around us.

There is no denying that since January 2021, over 3.3 million people have died worldwide from the COVID-19, and over one million of those are from the United States. As of today, there is a vaccine that has been made, but there is no known cure for the virus. Things are happening in our generation that has never happened before, no denying any of this. People are fearful and searching for answers.

However, I have good news for you and want to encourage your heart as a child of the Most High God. Know that the answer has been given to us if you only believe, and His name is Jesus.

You don't have to work for the covenant that has been established for you. You only have to accept what Jesus did for us by faith.

In the book of Psalm 23:4, it reads: "Yea, though I walk through the valley of the shadow of death, I will fear no evil: for thou art with me; thy rod and thy staff they comfort me."

I believe everyone is concerned about what our country and the world is experiencing right now, and rightly so. However, as a child of God, we should not walk in fear.

Second Timothy 1:7 tells us, "For God hath not given us the spirit of fear; but of power, and of love, and of a sound mind."

Not saying that fear will not try to come, because that is one of the devil's tricks and strategies. He wants to keep you from believing the Word of God so that you will be afraid to step out on faith. You must understand that your Redeemer lives.

> But when I am afraid, I put my trust in you.
> (Psalm 56:3 NLT)

We can go on and on in the Word of God, looking at His promises for our lives. But the question that we need to ask ourselves, because this is a personal decision that everyone has to make, is, Who do you say that He (Jesus) is?

The Word of God tells us in Matthew 9:29, "According to your faith be it unto you."

WOW (words of wisdom): I believe that the size of your faith determines the size of your God.

One of my favorite verses in the Bible is Psalm 9:10, and it says, "And they that know thy name will put their trust in thee: for thou, O LORD, hast not forsaken them that seek thee."

The war has already been fought and won. However, it is up to every person to prepare themselves for this journey and not protest the process.

With all the uncertainty surrounding our country and the world, I believe that we are at a time in our generation when God is asking this question to the people of God: Who do you say that I am?

The key to standing in God's righteousness and not protesting the process is this. You have to learn the good news that only the Word of God offers. You have to learn the price that was paid for you on the cross at calvary for your salvation. Furthermore, you have to learn God's way of living, apply and practice the principles that He has put in place for your life.

When you do, your faith will begin to grow. When your faith begins to grow, you will understand the authority that has been made available to you to use.

In the book of Proverbs 4: 20–22, God tells us, "My son, *attend* to my words [take charge of, to look after] incline thine ear unto my sayings. Let them not depart from thine eyes; keep them in the midst of thine heart. For they are life unto those that find them, and health to all their flesh" (emphasis mine).

God tells us in the book of John 6:63–64, "It is the spirit that quickeneth; the flesh profiteth nothing: the words that I speak unto you, they are spirit, and they are life. But there are some of you that believe not."

No matter what we are facing or what we will face in this life, God is asking His children (Christians) today the same question that He asked His disciples many years ago. Who do you say that I am? (Matthew 16:15).

Jesus asked many questions during His earthly ministry. That seemed to be one of His favorite teaching tools. The context of Jesus's question—Who do you say that I am?—is a very important question to all of us today.

When Jesus asked His disciples that question, He was provoking the disciples to consider their level of faith.

Romans 1:17 tells us, "The just shall live by faith." If there has ever been a time in our generation that we must have our faith in the finished work of the cross by the son of God, Jesus the Christ, the time is *now*! And we should not protest the process.

> Now the Holy Spirit tells us clearly that in the last times some will turn away from the true faith (what they believe); they will follow deceptive spirits and teachings that come from demons. (1 Timothy 4:1 NLT)

In response to the question that He asked the disciples, they responded based on several things they had heard. The crowds viewed Jesus as someone special, but their assumptions were wrong.

Many today (even some Christians) view Jesus as just someone special, but they only know Him from what others say He is to them, and don't know Him for themselves.

We must understand, as I stated earlier, that when Jesus asked the question "Who do you say that I am?" it wasn't for His benefit or knowledge, because He knew well the answer, but it was an example of His teaching methods that requires a response from us.

Everyone was created with a God-given awareness of Him. Romans 1:18 tells us that He put Himself into everybody's heart so that a man is without an excuse when they stand up in front of Him. But it is a difference in knowing about Him and knowing Him for yourself (having a personal relationship with Jesus).

As we study the written Word of God and learn who Jesus really is and the awesome price that He paid for us, we will be able to rightly answer this question.

Jesus paid the price for us by His grace so that we could get back our right standing with our Father God, because we lost that place during the fall of man.

When you know who Jesus is, you will understand why He came. Once you understand why He came, and you develop that personal relationship with Him, your life will never be the same. All of us that are born again, blood-bought children of God, are called to grow in faith.

Romans 10:17 tells us, "So then faith cometh by hearing, and hearing by the word of God."

> But ye beloved, build yourself up on your
> most holy faith, praying in the Holy Ghost.
> (Jude 1:20)

> But without faith it is impossible to please
> him: for he that cometh to God must believe that

he is, and that he is a rewarder of them that dili-gently seek him. (Hebrews 11:6)

WOW (words of wisdom): The size of your faith determines the size of your God.

Build your faith by the Word of God so that you can truly answer that question "Who do you say that I am?" When you do, you will be able to declare according to the Word of God who Jesus really is and who He is to you.

First Peter 3:15 tells us, "But sanctify the Lord God in your heart: and be ready always to give an answer to every man that asketh you a reason of the hope that is in you with meekness and fear."

When you have a relationship with Jesus, you can look back over your life and understand that if it had not been for the Lord on your side, you don't know where you would be. When you look back over your life, I believe that it should be easy to give someone a reason for the hope that you have.

So many Christians have accepted Jesus as their Savior but have never allowed Him to be their Lord. They have never developed a relationship with Him and don't have the correct answer to Jesus's question. God tells us in Hosea 4:6, "My people [Christians] are destroyed for a lack of knowledge."

There is always much more to know about Jesus. We will always be learning and growing in this life. The disciples had seen many miracles, including the raising of a widow's son (Luke 7: 11–17), the calming of a storm (Matthew 8:23–27), the casting out of many demons from a man (Matthew 8:28–34).

The disciples were part of the world's biggest fish fry that have not been broken, where Jesus feed over five thousand people with two fish and five loaves of bread (John 6:1–14).

However, they really didn't know who He was. Peter was the only one that answered the question from Jesus: Who do you say that I am?

Peter's reply: "Thou art the Christ, the Son of the living God." By Jesus's grace, He opened the other disciples' eyes to see Him for who He really was.

The disciples walked with Jesus; however, Jesus couldn't be everywhere at one time when He walked the earth with them. But now Jesus is as close to us as the mention of His name by His powerful Holy Spirit.

Romans 8:11 tells us, "But if the Spirit of him that raised up Jesus from the dead dwell in you, he that raised up Christ from the dead shall also quicken your mortal bodies by his Spirit that dwelleth in you."

If you do not protest the process, you will understand that in times of uncertainty, you will have comfort and hope in the midst of the tests and trials. Why, you may ask. You can have comfort because if God said it in His word, it's 100 percent guaranteed, and you know that it will come to pass.

God left us His living will for our life—the Holy Bible. It will teach you how to stand in the righteousness of God and how to release the authority that has been made available to us to use until we get to our final destination. The last thing He said was "It is finished."

When you make the wise decision to transform your mind by the powerful Word of God, He will show you who He is, and you will know who He is.

Numbers 23:19 AMP tells us, "God is not a man that He should lie, nor the son on man that He should repent. Has He said and will He not do it? Or has He spoken and will He not make it good and fulfill it?"

CHAPTER 4

Are You Properly Dressed?

As I look back and see how people took pride in how they carried themselves, I'm amazed at how people dress and carry themselves today. At an airport in the past, men would dress up in suits, and ladies would have on dresses. Oh, how things have changed. You rarely see shoeshine stands anymore, and so many are wearing shorts and flip-flops for shoes.

When I go to an appointment for business or take my wife out to dinner, a movie, or a walk in the park, I want to be properly dressed. I wouldn't wear what I just finished cutting the grass in or what I had on while working on the car when I am on a date with her. I know that she would still love me, but I would like to be properly dressed so that I don't embarrass her.

As it is in the nature, so it is in the spirit. As a child of the living God, if we are going to live in the victory that belongs to us until we get to our final destination, if we are going to have a successful Christian life now in this life, we have to be properly dressed.

God tells us in the book of Ephesians 6:10–13 (TLB):

> Last of all, I want to remind you that your strength must come from the Lord's mighty power within you. Put on all of God's armor so that you will be able to stand safe against all strategies and tricks of Satan. For we are not fight-

ing against people made of flesh and blood, but against persons without bodies—the evil rulers of the unseen world, those mighty satanic beings and great evil princes of darkness who rule this world; and against huge numbers of wicked spirits in the spirit world. So use every piece of God's armor to resist the enemy whenever he attacks, and when it is all over, you will still be standing up.

I pray that you can see yourself fully and properly dressed for battle.

I remember when I went into the military, there were fellow enlistees of all types with different backgrounds from all over the United States that wanted to serve our country. After signing up to serve in one of the different branches of the military (army, air force, navy, marines, reserve), you would be placed on a basic training camp.

By the time we all finished the boot camp of whatever branch we enlisted, we were all on one accord. We were all prepared for battle, no matter who we were, where we came from, or what background we had. What made the difference? It was the training that we received that prepared us to be *properly dressed* and able to fight the enemy. As it is in the natural, so it is in the spirit.

The armor of God, described by the Apostle Paul here in Ephesians 6:10–18, is our spiritual defense against the attacks of our enemy (the devil). Now if you were to leave home every morning wearing a full suit of armor, you would feel pretty silly, right? Thank God that's not necessary in this spiritual war that we are in. Although invisible, the armor of God is real, and when used properly and worn daily, it provides solid protection against the devil's (our enemy) attacks.

The body of Christ is in need of training today like never before in the history of our generation. We as Christians are supposed to be the army of God. We have to be *properly dressed* and trained to fight the good fight of faith in this war that we are in.

I know and talk to so many good Christians that are saved, love God, are on their way to heaven, but they are not enjoying the trip. I used to be like that. I was like a soldier marking time. I was moving or going through life, trying to figure life out, but wasn't going anywhere. God wants us to enjoy this trip because we are only going to pass this way but one time. However, you have to be *properly dressed* in order to do so.

WOW (words of wisdom): So many Christians have yet to understand that as a child of God, we are in a war that our eyes can't see.

So many Christians have yet to understand that we are not a human being going through a temporary spiritual experience; we are a spiritual being going through a temporary human experience.

Even if you are not a Christian, we all have the same makeup. We are a spirit, we have a soul, and we live inside a body.

Second letter to the Corinthians 10:3–5 tells us,

> For though we walk in the flesh, we do not war after the flesh: For the weapons of our warfare are not carnal, but mighty through God to the pulling down of strong holds, casting down imaginations, and every high thing that exalteth itself against the knowledge of God, and bringing into captivity every thought to the obedience of Christ.

Paul teaches us about the whole armor of God and how we need to put it on. When we obey this command, we will be *properly dressed* for battle against the devil (our enemy).

Notice this scripture says to put on the whole armor of God. Nowhere in the Word of God (The Bible) does it say to take it off. We should be *properly dressed* and have our spiritual armor on at all times. It should never be taken off so that we will be prepared and ready for battle at all times. We have to utilize every piece of God's armor as His soldiers every day.

Ephesians 6:13–17 says,

> Therefore take up the whole armor of God that you may be able to withstand in the evil day, and having done all, to stand. Stand therefore, having girded your waist with truth, having put on the breastplate of righteousness, and having shod your feet with the preparation of the gospel of peace; above all, taking the shield of faith with which you will be able to quench all the fiery darts of the wicked one. And take the helmet of salvation, and the sword of the Spirit, which is the word of God.

Our commander and chief (Jesus the Christ) has given us the battle plan on how to be *properly dressed* and how to stand our ground and win every time and in all situations.

However, you must understand. Although victory belongs to us as a child of God, it is not something that will just happen. You have to be trained to walk in victory because what level of victory we receive here on the earth is determined by the way we *properly dress* ourselves with the Word of the living God.

You have to know that we serve a good God. He came and took back everything that the first Adam lost so that we can have a right to the tree of life. John 10:10 tells us, "I am came that they might have life, and they might have it more abundantly" [in full measure].

You have to understand that just because it's God's will for us to be healthy, wealthy, and wise doesn't mean it's just going to be. If you don't *properly dress* yourself with the Word of God, the devil will keep you broke, busted, and disgusted all the days of your life. He will keep you unsure about the man named Jesus.

The war has already been fought and won. Jesus Christ has already won our victory through His sacrificial death on the cross (Revelation 1:18). However, to be *properly dressed*, we have to put on the effective armor that He has made available for us to win.

As we look at the different pieces of the armor Paul tell us about, none of these six pieces of armor require power on our part. However, if you are not *properly dressed* as a Christian, it is like having a flat tire on your car. If you don't change it and make the proper adjustment, you will not get very far. Jesus defeated every enemy when He died on the cross and conquered the grave three days later. It is from having confidence in His victory that you and I can put on the full armor of God and stand firm in our daily battles.

The belt of truth

The belt of truth is the first element of the armor of God. In the ancient world, a soldier's belt not only kept his armor in place but if wide enough, it protected his kidneys and other vital organs. So the truth of the Word of God protects us. Practically applied, you might say the belt of truth holds up our spiritual pants so that we're not exposed and vulnerable.

Jesus Christ called the devil the "father of lies." Deception is one of the enemy's oldest tactics. We can see through the devil's lies by holding them against the truth of the Bible (the Word of God). We must know this truth so that we can protect ourselves against the world, our flesh, and the father of lies (John 8:32).

The truth from the Word of God keeps us stable and reminds us of our identity in Christ. The Bible helps us defeat the lies of the devil that tries to tell us that money, materialism, and the pleasures of this world are the most important things in life. The devil is a lie.

Don't get me wrong, God wants us to have those things (but not the things having us). However, if you are not *properly dressed*, you will be out of balance.

In 1 Timothy 6:17, God tells us, "Charge them that are rich in this world, that they be not high minded, nor trust in uncertain riches, but in the living God, who giveth us richly all things to enjoy.

> Beloved, I wish above all things that thou
> may prosper and be in health, even as thou soul
> prosper. (3 John 2)

Fear not, little flock; for it is your father's
good pleasure to give you the kingdom. (Luke
12:32)

Everybody likes where it says in the Bible to ask and it shall be given. Seek and you shall find, knock and the door will be open, but Matthew 6:33 tells us, "But seek ye first the kingdom of God and His righteousness and all of the things shall be added."

You have to understand that the Word of God is conditional. If you are not properly dressed and don't understand the truth about things, it's not that you will not have things (money, materialism, and the pleasures of this world), but the things will have you.

But when you are *properly dressed*, the truth of God's Word shines its light of integrity into our lives and holds together all of our spiritual defenses.

The breastplate of righteousness

The breastplate of righteousness guards our heart. A wound to the chest can be fatal. That's why ancient soldiers wore a breastplate covering their heart and lungs.

Our heart is susceptible to the wickedness of this world, and we are truly living in a wicked world. However, our protection is the righteousness that comes from Jesus Christ. As a believer, we have no righteousness apart from that which has been given to us by Christ.

Our breastplate is His righteousness. His righteousness will never fail. No one is righteous in themselves but in Jesus. As His child, we are the righteousness of God in Christ Jesus.

Second Corinthians 5:21 tells us, "For he hath made him to be sin for us, who knew no sin; that we might be made the righteousness of God in him."

Proverbs 4:23 NLT says, "Guard your heart above all else, for it determines the course of your life."

The breastplate of righteousness symbolizes the righteousness we receive by believing in Jesus Christ.

Though we have no righteousness of our own, we must still, by God's power, choose to do right. Live a right life, rooted in God's word (Matthew 6:33). You cannot focus on the things of the world and all the immoral behavior which are not in line with your beliefs. Because when you do, it allows the devil to weaken the walls that Christ has built around you from His word. You have to identify unrighteous activities in your life that can weaken you.

When Jesus died on the cross, His righteousness was credited to all who believe in Him, through justification. God sees us as sinless because of what His Son Jesus did for us. Accept your Christ-given righteousness. Let it cover and protect you. Remember that it is His righteousness that will keep us in right standing with God.

Sandals with the gospel of peace

The gospel of peace is symbolized by sturdy, protective footwear.

Ephesians 6:15 talks about fitting our feet with the readiness that comes from the gospel of peace. In the ancient world, the terrain was rocky, requiring sturdy, protective footwear. On a battlefield or near a fort, the enemy might scatter barbed wire or sharp stones to slow an army down.

In the same way, the devil scatters traps for us as we're trying to serve God and be a light in dark places to spread the good news of the gospel. The gospel of peace is our protection, reminding us that we are secure in what Jesus has done for us.

Fitting our feet with the readiness of the gospel of peace is described in 1 Peter 3:15 like this: "But sanctify the Lord God in your hearts: and be ready always to give an answer to every man that asks you a reason of the hope that is in you with meekness and fear."

The easiest and most effective way to share the gospel (good news) with others is to tell your story of how Jesus changed your life.

Everyone has a story, and sharing your story and how God has changed your life allows you to share the gospel of salvation. This salvation will ultimately bring peace between God and man.

Romans 5:1 tells us, "Therefore being justified by faith, we have peace with God through our Lord Jesus Christ."

The way you live your life is the best example. When you carry yourself with the fruit of the spirit, people will stop and notice. I have learned that if you catch on fire for God, people will stop and watch you burn (they will take notice of your lifestyle). The world knows what Christians shouldn't do, but the world want to see how true Christians are supposed to live and carry themselves.

The shield of faith

Romans 1:17 tells us, "The just shall live by faith." Our faith in God's trustworthiness comes from the truth of the Bible.

Romans 10:17 tells us, "So them faith cometh by hearing and hearing by the word of God."

To the Roman soldier, no defensive armor was as important as the shield to a soldier. The shield fended off arrows, spears, and swords. Our shield of faith guards us against the devil's weapons that he tries to use against us.

One of the devil's deadliest weapons that he uses against us is doubt. The devil shoots doubt at us when we think God does not act immediately or visibly. Faith is the shield of the believer. Trusting in God's power and protection is imperative in remaining steadfast, unmovable, always abounding in the work of the Lord.

We know our Father (Jesus the Christ) can be trusted. Our shield of faith sends the devil's flaming arrows of doubt to fall to the ground and not affect us, when we are *properly dressed* with the Word of God. We must keep our shield held high, confident in the knowledge that God provides, God protects, and God is faithful to His children.

Second letter to Peter 1:2 tells us, "Grace and peace be multiplied unto you though the knowledge of God and of Jesus our Lord." Our shield of faith holds because of the One our faith is in, *Jesus Christ.*

The helmet of salvation

The helmet of salvation protects the head, where all thoughts and knowledge reside. It's an old saying that says if you kill the head, the body will fall. One blow to the head could prove fatal. The soldier's helmet covered his entire head, facial area, and between the eyes. The armor would be useless if he wasn't equipped with his helmet.

Jesus Christ said to the Jews who believed in Him in the book of John 8:31–32, "If ye continue in my word or hold on to my teaching, then are ye my disciples indeed; And ye shall know the truth, and the truth shall make you free."

The truth of salvation through Christ does indeed set us free. We are free from vain searching. Free from the meaningless temptations of this world, and free from the condemnation of sin. Romans 8:1 tells us, "There are now no condemnation to them which are in Christ Jesus, who walk not after the flesh, but after the spirit."

When you know, without a doubt, that you are going to heaven when this life is over because of what Jesus did on the cross, not even death can defeat you.

The helmet of salvation is to protect our thoughts and mind. It is a crucial piece of the armor. We cannot survive without it. The mind is the battlefield.

That's why it tells us in Romans 12:1–2,

> I beseech you therefore, brethren, by the mercies of God, that ye present your bodies a living sacrifice, holy, acceptable unto God, which is your reasonable service. And be not conformed to this world: but be ye transformed by the renewing of your mind, that ye may prove what is that good, and acceptable, and perfect, will of God.

Paul tells us in the book of Philippians 2:5, "Let this mind be in you that was also in Christ Jesus." We can't stop thoughts that are not of God from coming, but we have to cast them down.

Second Corinthians 10:5 NLT explains to us that those who are in Christ have divine power to demolish arguments and every pretension that sets itself up against the knowledge of God, and we can take captive every thought to make it obedient to Christ.

KJV says it like this: "Casting down imaginations, and every high thing that exalteth itself against the knowledge of God, and bringing into captivity every thought to the obedience of Christ."

First Corinthians 2:16 NLT tells us that believers have the mind of Christ. It says, "For, who can know the LORD's thoughts? Who knows enough to teach him? But we understand these things, for we have the mind of Christ."

Certainly, you are free to choose because God gave us a free will, but you are not free from the consequences of your choices. Those who reject God's plan of salvation battle the devil unprotected and suffer the fatal blow of hell when this life is over.

The sword of the Spirit

The sword of the Spirit represents the Bible (the Word of God), our weapon against the devil.

The sword of the Spirit is the only offensive weapon in the armor of God that we can use to fight against the devil and win.

It's the only weapon in the armor that we have to back the devil (our enemy) up off of us. This weapon represents the Word of God (the Bible) for the Word of God is alive and active.

In the book of Hebrews 4:12, it tells us, "For the word of God is quick, and powerful, and sharper than any two-edged sword, piercing even to the dividing of the soul and spirit, and of the joints and marrow, and it is a discerner of the thoughts and intents of the heart."

When Jesus was tempted in the wilderness by the devil, He defeated every temptation with the truth of Scripture, setting an example for us. The devil's tactics have not changed, so the sword of the Spirit (the word of God) is still our best defense.

The devil does not have any new tricks, just new faces, but his tricks are the same. There are many Christians that have not properly dressed themselves with the Word of God. When the devil comes at them, they pull their sword out, but it's dull.

It's dull because they don't know the Word of God. When the devil attacked Jesus in the wilderness, Jesus responded by saying, "For it is written." He told the devil what the word of God said concerning that area of His life.

In the book of Hosea 4:6, it says, "My people [Christians] are destroyed for a lack of knowledge." Jesus used scriptures to defeat the devil when He was tempted, and we as children of God must do the same if we want to win.

Matthew 13:11 tells us, "It is given to you to know the mysteries of the kingdom, but to them, it is not. They that see, see not and they that hear, hear not neither do they understand."

The power of prayer

Finally, Paul adds the power of prayer to the armor of God. Ephesians 6:18 tells us, "Praying always with all prayer and supplication in the Spirit, and watching thereunto with all perseverance and supplication for all saints."

> And pray in the Spirit on all occasions with
> all kinds of prayers and requests. With this in
> mind, be alert and always keep on praying for all
> of the Lord's people. (NLT)

Every smart soldier knows they must keep the line of communication open to their commander. God has orders for us through His Word and the promptings of the Holy Spirit. The devil hates it when we pray. He knows that prayer strengthens us and keeps us alert to his deception.

Paul cautions us to pray for others as well. With the armor of God and prayer, we can be ready for whatever the devil (our enemy) throws at us.

Jesus set the greatest example for us. When the devil (the tempter, our enemy) came to Him with temptations, He responded with the sword of the Spirit (the Word of God), which is a piece of our armor. So how much more are we to respond in the same way?

We must be *dressed properly* in order to respond properly. It is time for us as Christians to take an aggressive stand against the devil (our enemy). When we learn how to use every piece of the armor that has been made available to us by God, *we will win every battle every time.*

The Lord told me years ago that somebody has to demonstrate this walk of life. Although the war has been fought and won, we must fight the good fight of faith daily. Thankfully, we know with every fight we face, we have the armor and the weapons to help us defeat the enemy.

I'm a living witness that if you know, you will grow.

If you doubt, you will do without.

If you pray, you will stay.

If you fast, you will last.

If you are willing, God is able.

If you work the word of God, the word of God will work in your life.

If you can furnish the faith to believe, the Holy Spirit will do the work.

I want to encourage you to do whatever you need to do to be strong in the Lord and in the power of His might as a Christian. Put on the whole armor of God. Not just put it on but keep it on, and learn how to use it in your everyday walk of life.

Salvation is the best decision that we can make here on earth. If I don't wake up in the morning, I know that everything will be all right. But salvation only prepares us for heaven. It's how we live before we get there.

> For I am not ashamed of the gospel of Jesus
> Christ, for it is the power of God until salvation
> to everyone that believe it. (Romans 1:16)

Ponder [to think about very carefully, to meditate] the path of your feet, and let all your ways be established. (Proverbs 4:26)

Good understanding gives us favor, but the way of transgressors is hard [to break or violate, to do wrong, to sin]. (Proverbs 13:15)

For if we sin willfully after that we have received the knowledge of the truth, there remaineth no more sacrifice for sins. (Hebrews 10:26)

So examine yourself against the Word of God, and you will see if you are *properly dressed.*

CHAPTER 5

◇◇◇

This Battle Requires Action

Have you ever noticed that everywhere you look in the Bible, it advocates actions (a person or group that defends or maintains a cause)?

> Fight the good fight of faith. (1 Timothy 6:12)

> Resist the devil, and he will flee from you. (James 4:7)

> Take the sword of the spirit which is the word of God. (Ephesians 6:17)

> Study to show yourself approve unto God. (2 Timothy 2:15)

> Humble yourself in the sight of the Lord, and He shall lift you up. (James 4:10)

> If you are willing and obedient, you shall eat the good of the land, but if you refuse and rebel, you shall be devoured with the sword. (Isaiah 1:19–20)

> Very, very I say unto you, whatsoever you bind on earth shall be bound in heaven and whatsoever you loose on earth shall be loose in heaven. (Matthew 18:18)

> Work out your own salvation with fear and trembling. (Respect and obedience) (Philippians 2:12)

> Come unto me all ye that labor or heavy laden, and I will give you rest. (Matthew 11:28)

> Endure hardship as a good soldier. (2 Timothy 2:3)

As we can see from just a few verses in the Bible, we are required to respond with an action. Although John 10:10 tells us that God came so that we can have life and have it more abundantly, it still requires action or a response on our part.

Jesus has set us free from the law of sin and death by taking our place on the cross to get back what was lost at the fall of man.

It tells us in the book of John 8:36, "If the Son therefore shall make you free, you shall be free indeed."

God has prepared the way for us to get back in right standing with Him until we get to our final destination, but it's going to require some action on our part.

WOW (words of wisdom): You have to understand this. *Just because Jesus died so that we can have life and have it more abundantly doesn't mean it just going to happen automatically.*

I thank God that I'm saved. I thank God that if I don't wake up in the morning, that everything will be all right.

> By grace are you saved though faith; and not of yourself. It is the gift of God; not of works, lest any man should boast. (Ephesians 2:8–9)

WOW (words of wisdom): Salvation is the only free gift that you will receive in this life. Everything else will cost you something.

Although salvation is a free gift from God, it requires action on our part to receive it.

> That if you confess with your mouth the Lord Jesus, and shalt believe in your heart that God halt raised Him from the dead, thou shall be saved. 10v. For with the heart man believeth unto righteousness; and with the mouth confession is made unto salvation. (Romans 10: 9–10)

> For God so loved the world that He gave His only begotten son that whosoever believeth in Him shall not perish, but have everlasting life. (John 3:16)

> For whosoever shall call upon the name of the Lord shall be saved. (Romans 10:13)

Although Jesus came so that we can have life and have it more abundantly, so many Christians have yet to understand that the blood of Jesus was not just shed for us to go to heaven. It was also shed for us to be healed, delivered, prosperous, and set free from all the tricks, strategies, and attacks of the devil while we are here on earth.

Jesus tells us in the book of Revelation 1:18, "I am he that liveth; and was dead; and behold, I am alive for evermore, A-men; and have the keys of hell and of death."

Those that the Son have set free are free indeed (John 8:36). However, it's going to require some action on our part to stay free.

We are in a season when God wants His people to take their rightful place in the arena of battle. Although the war has been fought and won for us by Jesus, there will be some battles that we must fight in the spirit realm that will require some action.

You have to understand that, as children of God, we are in a war that our eyes can't see. We are not fighting against flesh and blood (each other). Paul tells us in the book of Ephesians 6 that we are fighting against principalities, powers, and rulers of the darkness of this world, spiritual wickedness in high places. That's why Paul says put on the whole armor of God, so we will be able to stand against all the tricks and strategies of the devil. Our action is that we have to build a personal relationship with God.

How do you build a relationship with someone? I'm glad you asked that question. You build a relationship with someone by spending time with that person.

You might say, How do I spend time with God? And I'm so glad you asked that question also. When you read the Bible or listen to the Bible on tape, CD, your phone, or whatever device you have, you are spending time with God.

When you read or listen to the Word of God, He is talking to you. He is telling you how much He loves you and the price that He paid for you. He is letting you know the covenant that has been established for you. From the first book in the Bible (Genesis) to the last book of the Bible (Revelation) is a love story. The Old Testament is a law covenant, and the New Testament is a grace covenant.

When you read the Word of God, He is letting you know what belongs to you as His child and how to get access to the promises. When you read the Word of God, He is letting you know how the devil and demons operate and how to identify your enemy.

> Be sober, be vigilant [careful]: because your
> adversary the devil, as a roaring lion, walking
> about, seeking whom he may devour (destroy).
> (1 Peter 5:8)

You must understand that the Bible is the Word of God, but it also has the words of the devil, demons, angels, and men both good and bad.

When you read the Bible, God is also letting us know how to identify your enemy and how to access the spiritual authority that has been made available for us to use. It is letting us know how to release that power until we get to our final destination. He is also letting us know that it will require some action on our part. That's what happens when you read the Word of God.

Now when you pray, you are talking to God.

Philippians 4:6–7 tells us to "be careful [anxious] for nothing; but in everything by prayer and supplication, with thanksgiving let your request be known unto God. And the peace of God, which passes all understanding, shall keep your heart and minds though Christ Jesus."

> Casting all your care upon Him; for He cares for you; Be sober, be vigilant; because your adversary the devil, as a roaring lion, walketh about, seeking whom he may devour. (1 Peter 5:7–8)

> Cast thy burden upon the Lord, and He shall sustain thee (support you); He shall never suffer the righteous to be moved. (Psalm 55:22)

God wants to have a personal relationship with each one of us. When we sing praise songs, we are worshipping God. He tells us in Psalm 100:4 to "enter His gates with thanksgiving and into His courts with praise; be thankful to him and bless his name."

> I will praise the name of God with a song; and will magnify Him with thanksgiving. (Psalm 69:30)

> Praise ye the Lord. O give thanks unto the Lord; for He is good; for His mercy endureth for ever. (Psalm 106:1)

The last five chapters in the book of Psalm start off with "Praise ye the Lord." The writer tells us in the last book of Psalm (chapter 150), "Let everything that has breath praise the Lord. Praise ye the Lord."

Psalm 22:3 tells us that God inhabits the praises of His people (to take up residence, to reside in, to set, to occupy as a home).

You have to understand that God only gets our praises. The Word of God is for us. The tithes and offerings are for the church so that the kingdom of God can continue to advance and so that we can do greater works in the kingdom. But God only gets our praises, and it's going to require some action on our part.

When you have a relationship with God, you will have confidence in Him that He will do just what He promised. Our action is that we have to build a relationship with God, which will allow us to trust Him when we are facing difficult and challenging times in our lives.

You see, it's easy to say with your mouth that you trust God when everything is going good. It's easy to say with your mouth that by His stripes, you are healed when you are walking around well. It's easy to say that your God will supply all of your needs when you have a pocket full of money, but that doesn't tell the real you.

The late Dr. Martin Luther King said it like this: "The ultimate measure of a man is not where he stands in moments of comfort and convenience, but where he stands at times of challenge and controversy."

In the book of 1 Samuel 17:34–37 is a familiar story of a young boy named David that faced and killed a giant named Goliath.

WOW (words of wisdom): anything in your life that is contrary to the Word of God is a giant, and it is going to require action on your part to defeat it.

I believe that one of the writers of the last five chapters, the psalmist David, had a relationship with God. I believe that God taught David to believe and understand that no matter how big the giant is in front of you, it will not be able to stop or defeat you.

David was the youngest of eight brothers. His three oldest brothers had joined King Saul's army. David stayed at home, and he took care of his father's sheep.

The Philistines and the Israelites army faced each other on opposite hills, with a valley between them. They were enemies with each other because they both wanted to put a piece of land under their political control.

The Philistines got the upper hand first, but then the Israelites became the primary force in the region. The Philistines, by nature, were an aggressive and controlling people; they had a reputation, which was the primary reason why the two people clashed.

Goliath was a Philistine champion, and he would come out in the valley every day and taunt the Israelites. He would say, "Why are you coming out here to fight? I am a Philistine champion, you are only servants of Saul."

Then he made a challenge. He said, "Send one of your men out to fight me. If he kills me, we will be your slaves, but if I kill him, you all will be our salves." When King Saul and the Israelites heard this, they were terrified, and no one man wanted the challenge.

Goliath was a champion warrior, and he was a giant man. It tells us that he was about eight and a half feet tall, and he probably weighed about four hundred to five hundred pounds.

One day, Jesse sent David to take a basket of bread and grain to his brothers, as they were in Saul's army. I don't know if it was his first time going, but when he got to the camp, the army had already left. Whatever the case may have been, David went where his brothers were, delivering the bread and grains. While he was there, David heard Goliath taunting the Israelites, and he heard the challenge that he made.

King Saul had a huge reward for the man who would challenge and kill Goliath. This was what the king would give to the man who would accomplish this feat: one of his daughters as his wife, and his family would never have to pay taxes.

After hearing about the reward, David questioned some more of the men to make sure that's what King Saul had said. All of them agreed that was the reward. Then David said, "Don't worry about this Philistine, I will go and fight him."

The word got back to King Saul that they had a man who wanted to take the challenge. When the king saw David, he said, "Don't be ridiculous. Have you seen this giant? This man has been a man of war since his youth. You are only a boy."

It's an old saying that you can't judge a book by its cover. I can tell you some stories about how I have been judged because of the color of my skin, the way I used to dress, and because of the way I talk (pronunciation of some of my words). Dr. King said that he hopes that one day we would be able to live in a country where a man will not be judged by the color of his skin but by the content of his character (a group of qualities that make a person, group, or thing different from others). I thank God that He doesn't look on the outside; He looks at the heart.

WOW (words of wisdom): Another thing that God has taught me that you should know about this life is that you should never compare your life to anyone else's because you don't know what that person's journey is all about.

David told King Saul, "I have been taking care of my father's sheep and goats. When a lion or bear comes and steal one of them, I go after it and rescue it from its mouth. I will do the same thing to this Philistine, for he has defied the armies of the living God."

David said, "The Lord, who rescued me from the claws of the lion and bears, will rescue me from this Philistine."

King Saul finally consented and said to David, "May the Lord be with you." King Saul even gave David his armor.

David put it on and, after taking a few steps, said, "I can't go battle in this," and he took it off.

David picked up five smooth stones from a stream and put them in his shepherd's bag. He had only a shepherd's staff and his sling, and he went to the valley to fight the giant. In the natural, that didn't make much sense, but God tells us in the book of 1 Corinthians 1:27, "But God hath chosen the foolish things of the world to confound the wise and God hath chosen the weak things of the world to confound the things which are mighty."

I have heard many reasons why David picked up five stones. I believe that the five smooth stones David had in his pouch represented what I believe David had in his heart.

I believe David had

1) <u>faith,</u>

2) <u>trust,</u>
3) <u>courage,</u>
4) <u>obedience, and</u>
5) <u>praise.</u>

I believe that whenever we face any kind of giant in our lives, we can carry these five things with us in our heart and also receive the victory.

- Faith—"Now faith is the substance of things hope for, the evidence of things not seen" (Hebrews 11:1).
- Trust—"Trust in the Lord with all thine heart and lean not unto our own understanding. In all of our ways acknowledge Him, and He shall direct our steps" (Proverbs 3: 5–6).
- Courage—"Have I not commanded you to be strong and of good courage. Be not afraid neither be thou dismayed for the Lord thou God is with you whithersoever thou goest" (Joshua 1:9).
- Obedience—"Obedience is better than sacrifice" (1 Samuel 15:22).
- Praise—"Praise ye the Lord. O Give thanks to the Lord, for He is good and for His mercy endures forever" (Psalm 106:1).

David had a relationship with God, and he was confident that the same God that had protected him from the lions and bears would protect him from this giant.

When you are facing a situation (battle) in your life, just look back and see where the Lord has brought you from and how He has protected you in the past. Encourage yourself in the Lord your God. You can say, "Lord, I know you didn't bring me through that not to take me through this."

David was a man of faith. We just read about David's boldness, but I wanted to go to the root to see why David was so confident. I learned in my studies that the lions that David fought when he was protecting his father's sheep were the African lions which once inhabited most of the Middle East, including Israel, modern-day Turkey, etc.

It says that the mature male African lion was, on average, eight to nine feet from their nose to their rump, not including the tail. And the average weight was around 550 to 600 pounds.

The bear David fought was like the Eurasian brown bear. It has disappeared from much of its ancient range. This bear is almost identical to the grizzly bear of our time, and the adult brown bear could range from 900 to 1,200 pounds. The height of this bear is from nine to ten feet tall when standing up.

When you consider all of this together, we can see why David was so confident in the Lord. Out of all three—Goliath, the lion, and the bear—Goliath was like a midget.

The time came, and David went out to fight Goliath, and he said to David, "You think I am a dog, and you only come at me with a stick. I will give your flesh to the birds and wild animals."

David answered and said, "You come to me with a sword, a spear, and with a shield, but I come to you in the name of the Lord of heaven. Today the Lord will conquer you, and I will kill you. I will cut your head off, and the whole world will know that there is a God in Israel." Although David believed and meant what he said, it required some action on his part.

God is looking for us to take action because the only fight we are supposed to be fighting is the good fight of faith. God is looking for us to take Him at His Word and to line up with His Word.

Like I said, we are in a war that our eyes can't see. We are in a spiritual battle, and it requires some action on our part. God has given us His Word so that we can train ourselves to face the giants. These giants come in our lives and try to get us to give up in the battle.

Second Timothy 2:26 let us know that God gave us His word so that we can recover ourselves out of the snare of the devil, who are taken captive by him at his will. Anything that is contrary to the Word of God is a giant in your life, and it is going to require some action on your part to stand against it and defeat it.

God has given us everything we need to live in victory. Ephesians 1:3 tells us, "Blessed be the God and Father of our Lord and Savior, who has blessed us with all spiritual blessing in heavenly places in Christ Jesus."

We have everything we need to live in victory until we get to our final destination, but it's going to require some action on our part.

There are so many today who want to be classified as being a Christian, but their lifestyle and convictions are far from God's teachings and His truths.

The first thing you have to do to gain victory is to accept Jesus as your Savior. Then you have to learn His way of living and apply His principles to your life. When you apply the Word of God (principles) to your life, or when you work the Word of God in your life, your life will never be the same. I promise you.

This walk of life is going to require some action on our part. The last thing God said after He let them hang Him high and swing Him wide and before He took His last breath for you and for me was "It is finished."

God tells us in Matthew 16:18, "And I say also unto thee. That thou are Peter, and upon this rock I will build my church; and the gates of hell shall not prevail against it."

That means that the resistance of the devil to maintain his ground in your life will not *prevail* (succeed; win control over) against you when you commit to the things of God. You must first understand it's going to require some action on your part.

CHAPTER 6

Knowledge Bills, Wisdom Fills, and Understanding Establishes

Matthew 15:6 tells us, because of tradition, the Word of God has no effect in your life.

You have to understand and believe that no matter what's going on in the world today, the same God that has protected, provided, and made provisions for us in the past is the same God today. I have learned in my walk with the Lord that hard times don't change God. He tells us in the book of Malachi 3:6, "For I am the Lord, I change not."

Hebrews 13:8 tells us, "Jesus Christ the same yesterday, and today and forever."

I have learned on my journey that hard times don't change God; however, I have also learned that hard times should change the way a person thinks about life and make the proper adjustments that's necessary.

Don't believe me; always believe the Word of God.

A prudent [cautious] person foresees the danger ahead and takes precautions; the simple [ordinary] person goes blindly on and suffers the consequences. (Proverbs 22:3 NLT)

I found out that Jesus is the wisest man I know, and He tells us in the book of John 8:12 that He is the light of this world and he that followeth after Him shall not walk in darkness, but shall have the light of life. I know that the world seems to be covered with a lot of darkness, but there is hope.

Not only that, I want to give you the uncut version of the gospel and to sell the devil out. That fool tried to kill me. After being in a military accident where the doctors gave me very little hope of survival, I had nothing to stand on or depend on but God and His word.

After having an out-of-body experience, when God put me back in my flesh, I had to learn how to do everything over. The doctors deemed me incompetent, and I had to have someone during that period of time handle all my affairs because I wasn't able to do for myself.

My first book, *From the Pigpen to the Pulpit*, featuring my out-of-body experience, will give you more details about my testimony and what had happened to me during that time.

I was in a very bad place in my life at that time and couldn't understand what had happened. I knew a lot of God's promises concerning healing and what He died for me to have in this life. That was the only thing that gave me hope. No matter what things seemed to look like around me, I had my hope and faith in the finished work of the cross by Jesus the Christ.

I want to let you know that when you put your trust in God and stand on His promises for your life, He will show you that everything that the devil means for your bad, He will turn them around for your good by His grace. I can be bold in my declaration because I am a living testament of His miraculous power.

Hosea 4:6 NLT tells us, "My people [Christians] are destroyed for lack of knowledge because they don't know me. Because thou hast rejected knowledge, I will also reject thee, that thou shalt be no priest to me: seeing thou hast forgotten the law of thy God, I will also forget thy children."

Solomon wrote these words in the book of Ecclesiastes:

> I have observed something else under the sun. The fastest runner doesn't always win the race, and the strongest warrior doesn't always win the battle. The wise sometimes go hungry, and the skillful are not necessarily wealthy. And those who are educated don't always lead successful lives. It is all decided by time and chance. People can never predict when hard times might come. Like fish in a net or birds in a trap, people are caught by sudden tragedy. Here is another bit of wisdom that has impressed me as I have watched the way our world works. There was a small town with only a few people, and a great king came with his army and besieged it. A poor, wise man knew how to save the town, and so it was rescued. But afterward no one thought to thank him. So even though *wisdom* is better than strength, those who are wise will be despised if they are poor. What they say will not be appreciated for long. It is better to hear the quiet words of a wise person than the shouts of a foolish king. It is better to have wisdom than weapons of war, but one sinner can destroy much that is good. (Ecclesiastes 9:11–18 NLT; emphasis mine)

> Wisdom is the principal thing; therefore get wisdom: and with all thy getting get understanding. Exalt her, and she shall promote thee: she shall bring thee to honor, when thou dost embrace her. (Proverbs 4:7–8)

> Good understanding gives favor, but the way of transgressors is hard [to break or violate, to do wrong, to sin]. (Proverbs 13:15)

As we look at the world today, nobody predicted that we would be living through what's going on in our generation. Nobody predicted that we would be in a historical event that would go down in the history books for generations to come.

No one knew that there would be a global pandemic that has been named the coronavirus or COVID-19. At the time of this writing, no one knew that it would have killed over 1.3 million people globally. In addition, over 900,000 people have died from this virus just in the United States alone, and the numbers continue to rise.

They say that the economy was doing so good. But today, as I write this book, this country has been at a standstill. It was shut down and is now trying to get back to a new norm. The latest information that I heard from CNN, when the virus first began, was that in less than a month, over 26.5 million people had lost their jobs and filed for unemployment. And again, the numbers keep going up.

I have seen on TV where so many have lined up for miles and waited for hours just to get food. So many are living in fear because they don't know how their bills are going to get paid.

You might not have the virus, and I hope you are praising God for His protection, but we are in a world now where so many people are stressed out and looking for answers.

We are living in a generation with diseases no man can heal and with problems that no man can solve. We are living in a generation today where wrongs are being called right and rights are being called wrong. And people are searching for answers. This is truly a challenging time for many Americans

Second letter to Timothy 3:1 says, "Know this also, that in the last days perilous times shall come." I believe that we can agree that we are now living in some hard times. (Can I get an amen?)

I have found out on this journey, and whether you realize it or not, that so many people today don't want to hear the truth. But John 8:32 tells us, "And you shall know the truth, and the truth shall make you free."

I have been mandated by God to tell you the truth so you can have the choice to accept it or reject it. If I don't tell you the truth, then I am rejecting it for you.

For everything that is going on in the world today, I want to submit to you that the only true answer about the matters we are facing is *Jesus Christ*.

Because it's hard to understand the depths of what Jesus did on the cross for us, so many people (even many Christians) fail to live up to the privileges that are theirs as a child of God. Why, you may ask? It is because many Christians have not prepared themselves by applying the Word of God to their life.

It's true that the Christian life begins with Jesus, but there's more to this life than just accepting Jesus as your Savior. I do believe that our background and our circumstances may have an influence on who we are, but when we became a Christian, a child of the living God, we are responsible for who we become.

Paul tells us, and it can't be emphasized enough. In the book of Romans 12:1–2,

> I beseech you therefore, brethren by the mercies of God, that ye present your bodies a living sacrifice, holy, acceptable unto God, which is your reasonable service. And be not conformed to this world: but be ye transformed by the renewing of your mind, that ye may prove what is that good, and acceptable, and perfect, will of God.

Philippians 2:5 tells us to "let this mind be in you, which was also in Christ Jesus."

I have learned that so many people think that if you just believe in Jesus, you will experience all the depths of joy that God has promised. However, that's not the case. Because of a lack of knowledge that I had, I thought that Jesus was going to do everything for me.

Yes, Jesus took our place on the cross and died to get back everything that the first Adam lost. Yes, He died so that we can have life and have it more abundantly, but it's not an automatic process. You and I have a part to play in our walk with the Lord.

Romans 15:4 tells us, "For whatsoever things were written aforetime were written for our learning, that we though patience and comfort of the scripture might have hope."

People are looking for hope today, but do not understand that our only hope is Jesus. Jesus tells us in the book of John 16:33, "These things I have spoken unto you, that in me ye might have peace. In the world ye shall have tribulation: but be of good cheer; I have overcome the world."

So many people in the world today are trying to make it without God; they are building their lives in their own strength and ability. But God tells us in the book of Zechariah 4:6, "Not by might, nor by power, but by my spirit, saith the lord of host."

> The Glory of this latter house shall be
> greater than the former, saith the Lord of hosts:
> and in this place will I give peace, saith the Lord
> of hosts. (Haggai 2:9)

God does tell us that our latter shall be greater than our former, but we have to prepare for our latter. Many people don't want to prepare their life with God in the center. They want God to be around their life instead of building their life around God's teachings or His way of living.

Second letter to Peter 1:2 tells us, "Grace and peace be multiplied unto you though the knowledge of God, and of Jesus our Lord."

That's why knowledge bills, wisdom fills, and understanding establishes.

Those who build their lives on the Word of God will have security or stability no matter what's going on in the world. Those who reject God's teachings and try to build their lives by the world's system will not be able to stand the pressures of this life.

Let me encourage you in knowing that blessed is the man who walks in the wisdom of the Lord.

Psalm 1 tells us,

> Blessed is the man that walketh not in the counsel of the ungodly, nor standeth in the way of sinners, nor sitteth in the seat of the scornful. But his delight is in the law of the Lord; and in his law doth he meditate day and night. And he shall be like a tree planted by the rivers of water, that bringeth forth his fruit in his season; his leaf also shall not wither; and whatsoever he doeth shall prosper. The ungodly are not so: but are like the chaff which the wind driveth away. Therefore the ungodly shall not stand in the judgment, nor sinners in the congregation of the righteous. For the Lord knoweth the way of the righteous: but the way of the ungodly shall perish.

It's an old saying, "Give a man a fish; he will eat for a day. Teach a man how to fish, and he will eat for a lifetime." Dr. Joseph says it like this: Give a man a Word from God, and he will be inspired for a day. Teach a man how to hear from God, and he will be inspired for a lifetime.

It is only by faith in the all-powerful God that we can be superior to circumstances and be victorious over all the evil forces that would try to destroy us.

Look at this COVID-19 virus that's out in the world today. It doesn't discriminate. It doesn't care anything about you, where you are from, if you are Black, White, Asian, Chinese, or how much money you have. Not only that, this virus has no respecter of persons.

John 10:10 tells us, "The thief [devil] comes not but to steal, kill and to destroy."

As it is in the natural, so it is in the spirit.

Jesus is the same way. He doesn't discriminate. He doesn't care where you are from, if you are Black, White, Asian, Chinese, or how much money you have. But He does care about your soul and everything that concerns you, and He is the one that came to give you life and life more abundantly (John 10:10).

I understand people today who are carrying the message that Jesus loves you, and the message that he died for you is offensive to society. However, Jesus is still waiting and wanting to be your Savior. He is waiting for you to ask Him into your heart and be Lord over your life.

Psalm 33:12 says, "Blessed is the nation whose God is the Lord."

Jesus is still Lord; however, so many people have rejected God and His plan for their life. Furthermore, there are many that are trying to put Him out of this nation.

I believe the first reason why this country has been losing the culture and the moral values that it was founded on (which is the Word of God) is very simple. We the people have separated ourselves and our nation from God.

As this country became more prosperous as a nation, so many have become less dependent on God. When you compromise the Word of God, you ask God to leave.

Back in the fifties, Americans had just modified the Pledge of Allegiance that included "one nation under God." I remember that it was something we would say in school every morning.

"I pledge *allegiance* to the flag of the United States of America and to the Republic for which it stands, one Nation under God, indivisible, with liberty and justice for all."

And it was during that time our national motto "In God we trust" was adopted. The Bible and prayer was welcome in schools. But oh how things have changed.

We are living in a world today where that same God is not welcome in our schools anymore. We are living in a world today where Christians have to fight for the right to mention the name of Jesus. Furthermore, we are living in a world today where Christians that want to live out their faith in every area of their life are under attack.

So many are wondering what's going on in the country. You have to understand that when you compromise the Word of God and don't stand for the things that God stands for, you are asking Him to leave.

No matter what things seem to look like in our nation, there is good news. We that are blood-bought children of God have been redeemed from the curse of the law. Galatians 3:13 tells us, "Christ hath redeemed us from the curse of the law, being made a curse for us: for it is written, Cursed is every one that hangeth on a tree."

In John 15: 5, Jesus tells us, "I am the vine, ye are the branches: He that abideth in me, and I in him, the same bringeth forth much fruit: for without me ye can do nothing."

It's an old saying that says "You can lead a horse to water, but you can't make him drink it, or you can't drink it for him."

The Lord instructed me over twenty-five years ago to tell the people of God to start preparing themselves. He instructed me to encourage His people to study His Word and to learn the covenant that has been established for us. He told me to tell His people to begin saving money.

My mama used to tell me as a kid that it is better to have money and not need it than to need money and not have it.

God told me to tell people over twenty-five years ago that the world system was going to shut down, and the only thing that is going to keep us protected and what we could depend on is the covenant that He has established for His people.

I thought in 2001 after 9/11 that people would see the decline in our nation and this country needed to change. Churches were full of people for about two months and then people went back to their way of living, and this country got worse.

Then in 2008, when the financial collapse took place, I thought that was what the Lord was talking about when He instructed me to tell the people that the world system was going to shut down. He also wanted me to let them know how important it was to be prepared. To draw close to Him because He is the only one who promises to supply all of our needs according to His riches in glory by Christ Jesus.

As I was praying to God, when the pandemic started in our country and around the world, He told me that the events in 2001 and 2008 were just signs to show people how important it was to be prepared for the unexpected. To be prepared not only spiritually

(2001) but to also be prepared financially (2008) for a time such as this.

I don't believe there was anyone that left home the morning of 9/11 in the year of 2001 who knew that they were going to meet their Creator that day.

But as I watched and listened, stayed the course that God had put me on, I continued to tell the people to prepare themselves, but so many of them did not. In 2008, I saw so many large corporations like banks, airlines, and big tech companies depending on our government to bail them out from the financial collapse. However, we as the people of God, that depend on the *knowledge*, *wisdom*, and *understanding* of the Lord, will be able to stand the test of time in these evil days.

I believe I know how Noah felt when God told him to build the ark. To tell the people that it was going to rain and nobody listened to him, but he stayed the course. For 120 years, nobody listened. They made fun of him and didn't prepare themselves. They talked and laughed about him, but at the end of the day, when it started to rain, only he and his family were saved (Genesis 5:32–10:1).

God wants to perform all of His promises through our life as a child of His, but there is only one way to get them. It's His way or no way.

> I am the way the truth and the life, no man cometh to the Father but by me. (John 14: 6)

> I know that the way of man is not in himself. It is not in man that walketh to direct his steps. (Jeremiah 10:23)

> There is a way that seems right unto a man, but the end thereof are the ways of death. (Proverbs 16:25)

> Behold I was brought forth in iniquity, and in sin my mother conceived me. (Psalm 51:5)

If you have not received Jesus as your personal Savior, then you will not receive the promises that are yours as a child of God. However, when you accept Jesus as your Lord and Savior, you put a seal on your salvation, and you become a citizen of heaven, but you also gain the rights to have anything heaven offers right here on earth.

It is written—"Thou kingdom come, thou will be done in earth as it is in heaven."

Everybody wants to go to heaven, when God is trying to get heaven on earth.

You can position yourself by the Word of God and make up your mind to live on earth as it is in heaven. If you work the Word of God, you have a heavenly account, and you can make a withdrawal from it now in this life.

I have positioned myself by the Word of God and have made up in my mind to live on earth as a kingdom citizen. Jesus said, "Thou kingdom come, thou will be done on earth as it is in heaven."

The Word of God declares I could be blessed when I come, and I could be blessed when I go, blessed in the city and blessed in the field. I could be the head and not the tail, above only and not beneath. The Word says that when my enemies that rise up against me one way, they will have to flee seven ways (Deuteronomy 28:6–7).

> So shall they fear the name of the LORD from the west, and his glory from the rising of the sun. When the enemy shall come in like a flood, the Spirit of the LORD shall lift up a standard against him. (Isaiah 59:19)

First letter to Timothy 6:17 tells us, "Charge them that are rich in this world, that they be not highminded, nor trust in uncertain riches, but in the living God, who giveth us richly all things to enjoy."

People say that Jesus was poor. Tradition or religion says that you are supposed to walk around looking poor, barely making it, and if you live like that, it shows humility. The devil is a lie. If that's the way you want to live, I am not mad at you. God is not mad at you, but you will never enjoy the finer things in this life that belongs to you before you get to your final destination.

If all your talk is about Jesus, and you say that He is the great I am that I am, but you are always broke busted and disgusted, I don't know anyone who wants to serve that kind of God. Let me explain something. It's not about having things just for the sake of being prosperous, but all throughout the Word of God, we see a generous God who always abundantly blesses His people. However, He desires that we walk in His will and His ways.

Second letter to the Corinthians 8:9 says, "For ye know the grace of our Lord Jesus Christ, that, though he was rich, yet for your sakes he became poor, that ye through his poverty might be rich."

Third letter to John 2 tells us, "Beloved, I wish above all things that thou mayest prosper and be in health, even as thy soul prospereth."

> See then that you walk circumspectly [careful] not as fools but as wise. Redeeming the time because the days are evil. Wherefore be not unwise but understanding what the will of the Lord is. (Ephesians 5:15–17)

Acting on the Word of God takes believing the Word. Speaking the Word of God takes knowing the Word. The Word of God is the foundation to gaining greater power by the blood of the lamb (Jesus Christ).

People who don't feed on the Word of God are people who have trouble following God. People who don't read the Word of God are like a blind man that want to read and can't see.

Knowledge bills, wisdom fills, and understanding establishes.

Because life doesn't give you many second chances. *The opportunity of a lifetime must be seized in the lifetime of the opportunity.* The Word of God is only going to work in our life when we work the Word.

Joshua 1:8 tells us, "This book of the law shall not depart out of thy mouth; but thou shalt meditate therein day and night, that thou mayest observe to do according to all that is written therein: for then thou shalt make thy way prosperous, and then thou shalt have good success."

Proverbs 4:26 tells us, "Ponder [to think about very carefully, to meditate] the path of your feet, and let all your ways be established."

If you have been living contrary to the Word of God, you can begin today to let your ways be established. You have to start somewhere if you want God's results.

If you have never accepted Jesus as your Savior so that when this life is over He will welcome you into His kingdom, you have that opportunity right now to ask Him to come into your heart and be your Savior.

As we can see from this global pandemic that has taken over 1.3 million lives, and the numbers are still going up, it should remind us that life is but a vapor.

James 4:14 tells us, "Whereas ye know not what shall be on the morrow. For what is your life? It is even a vapour, that appeareth for a little time, and then vanisheth away."

Furthermore, I leave you with this WOW (word of wisdom) that will never change: knowledge bills, wisdom fills, and understanding establishes.

CHAPTER 7

The Ball Is in Your Court

A poem writer wrote a poem, and one of the lines says, "It matters not how straight the gate or how charge [to give full responsibility to] with punishment the scroll. I am the master of my fate [predetermine events]; I am the captain of my soul."

No believer (Christian) can live in separation from the world. As a child of God that has transformed their mind by the Word of God, we now understand that we are not of the world but we are in the world.

God has decreed His word (things decided) for each of our lives. However, we can only go so far in our own strength and ability. But the good news is we don't have to go in our own strength and ability. In the Word of God, we have everything we need, but there are rules that must be followed to receive what God has planned for our life.

> If ye be willing and obedient, ye shall eat
> the good of the land: But if ye refuse and rebel, ye
> shall be devoured with the sword: for the mouth
> of the Lord hath spoken it. (Isaiah 1:19–20)

> But seek ye first the kingdom of God, and
> his righteousness; and all these things shall be
> added unto you. (Matthew 6:33)

We are only going to pass this way but one time, and we are only going to get one chance at this walk of life. You have to know how to play (walk out and live this life according to the Word of God).

We are all playing the same game. It's called the game of life, but I thank God for making a way so that we can all be winners. *The ball is in your court* because God has accomplished everything for us by His death, burial, and His resurrection.

The key is not the will to win in this life; everybody has that. The key is the will to prepare ourselves to win—that's important. Although victory belongs to us as a child of God, we have a choice to dribble, shoot, or pass (living our life according to the Word of God) if we want to win in this life.

Some people receive knowledge but reject revelation. The amount of revelation that you receive is determined by how close you want to walk with God. The Word of God tells us how to live, but some people refuse to accept it and don't want to follow God and His plan for their lives.

You can know the Word of God and still not act upon it. Jesus is not truly Lord over your life until you respond to His teachings. However, from the day you start to build a proper spiritual foundation, you will see the blessing of God in every area of your life.

In the world that we live in today, there are so many that are trying everything the world has to offer except for the way God has designed for us to live.

- Many today still think they can find peace of mind in pills.
- They try to eat their way to ecstasy.
- They try to smoke their way to settle their nerves.
- They try to drink their way to pleasure.
- They try to puff their way to popularity, and they try to push their way to power, to live.

I learned as a child that no one owes you anything. I was raised in a generation where if you wanted something, you worked for it. You had to go and work hard to get it for yourself.

That was easy for me to understand because from the time that I can remember, all I knew was to work hard. We had to work hard to have food on the table. We had to work hard to cut wood so that Mama could cook our meals and keep the house warm in the winter. Not only that, we had to work hard to survive.

When I moved away from home to a big city, there were times when I had to work up to three jobs at one time, trying to survive. I knew about God because my mother raised us all in the church. However, the God that they preached about in the church I grew up in, I didn't want a relationship with that kind of God and accept Him as my Savior.

All I heard preached about God was fear instead of faith. Instead of teaching you about God's goodness and His mercy, they preached that everything you did wrong would send you to hell. I knew in my heart that God had all the right answers, but I never had anyone to tell me or show me the right answers about God.

I didn't know the Word of God at that time for myself; I only knew what I thought was the truth, to find out later that it wasn't. All I knew was that the ball was in my court. As a grown man now, I had to work hard for everything that I wanted.

I was working hard trying to make it. Trying to live a good, clean life. I had not accepted Jesus as my personal Savior yet, because of my upbringing and the preaching I heard about this man named Jesus.

I worked hard, not asking anyone to do anything for me. I didn't know much about taxes at that time. Not only that, I thought that if you work hard and not depend on the government system, you could work as much as you want without being penalized.

During that time, I remember receiving a letter from the IRS telling me that I made too much money, and I owed over $4,000 in taxes. I learned as a child that nobody owes you anything, so how can I owe the government money? I called the IRS and asked several questions about the letter that I received, and wanted someone to explain to me how a poor man can make too much money.

Another lesson that I've learned is that a man without God will break his health down trying to make it in this life, to survive and get wealth, and then later in life turn around and spend all of his wealth trying to get his health back.

I want you to know that with God on your side, it doesn't have to be like that. After going down the road of hard knots, trying to make it by myself, I came to a point in my life when I couldn't even think of anything to try that might work. I had tried everything but God, and that is when I asked Him to come into my life and be my Savior.

After I learned God's way of doing things, and after applying His principles to my life, I came to realize that *"for to me to live is Christ, and to die is gain"* (Philippians 1:21).

After looking back over my life and the way that I was raised, I can tell you from experience where a poor man has a chance.

I know where a sick man can get well.

I can tell you where an ignorant man can become wise.

I can tell you where a blind man can receive his sight.

I can tell you where a bad man can be made good, and a good man can be made better.

I even know where a dead man can be made alive.

The answer is in Jesus Christ.

You see, when we live unto the Lord, when we die, we die unto the Lord.

The Lord told me over twenty-five years ago that somebody has to stand for the things of God because everybody can't fall.

This book is to present a supernatural help to all people with symptoms that the doctor says are incurable. Medical science tells us there are many incurable diseases such as some forms of cancer, arthritis, heart disease, and AIDS, just to name a few.

This book is about the supernatural Word of God (when you know who Jesus is). God's Word is supernatural. Mixing your faith with God's Word by speaking it out of your mouth is a means of applying God's medicine.

The purpose of this writing is to reveal principles from God's Word. Also, to teach you how to cooperate with God's Word and apply these principles to obtain healing. I can share with you from the Word of God, but the only thing I can't do is do it for you. It is up to the individual whether they have the confidence to take God's medicine (the Word of God) daily.

Let me say this and put it on paper: I'm not teaching against doctors or medicine, but don't depend on that alone to keep you healthy.

There are some diseases that medical science cannot cure. If you need a doctor, see a doctor. Many lives are saved every year though medical help. There are medicines today that are beneficial in aiding the body's healing process. Your body was created with the ability to heal itself, and if every part functions properly, it will.

I am convinced from my own experience that your words are vital to your health and well-being. I believe that there are some diseases that will never be cured unless people learn to speak the language of health that the body understands.

Many people today are seeking healing; however, they talk sickness and suffering until they establish that image in them. Their thoughts and words produce a vivid blueprint, and they live within the bounds and limitations of that blueprint.

I want to show you how to make your blueprint line up with the Word of God.

In the book of Proverbs 18:21, it tells us, "Death and life are in the power of the tongue: and they that love it shall eat the fruit thereof." What you believe and speak not only affects your body but it affects your immune system as well. Your words are either a blessing or a curse to you.

Your words are building blocks of which you construct your life and future. Words set the cornerstones of your life, and you live within the confines of that boundary you create with your own words. Situations, circumstances, and conditions are all subject to change, but with the support of your words, you can establish them in your life forever.

Matthew 12:37 tells us, "For by thy words thou shalt be justified, and by thy words thou shalt be condemned."

A continual affirmation of God's Word in faith will build into your immune system a supernatural anointing that is capable of eliminating sickness and disease in a natural manner.

Jesus put it this way in the book of Luke 6:45: "A good man out of the good treasure of the heart bringeth forth that which is good; and an evil man out of the evil treasure of his heart bringeth forth that which is evil: for out of the abundance of the heart his mouth speaketh."

Like I said, I am convinced from my own experience that your words are vital to your health and well-being. You can't deny that something is wrong with you sometimes, and you can't help how you feel, but you can help what you say and what you do.

When God's Word is infused (engrafted) into you, and by giving voice to His word with your own mouth, this is the language of health to your body. Lining up with the Word of God is voice activated.

Here are a few of many scriptural reasons why I believe this so strongly.

> Thou shalt also decree a thing, and it shall
> be established unto thee: and the light shall shine
> upon thy ways. (Job 22: 28)

> A fool's mouth is his destruction, and his
> lips are the snare of his soul. (Proverbs 18:7)

> For verily I say unto you, That whosoever
> shall say unto this mountain, Be thou removed,
> and be thou cast into the sea; and shall not doubt
> in his heart, but shall believe that those things
> which he saith shall come to pass; he shall have
> whatsoever he saith. (Mark 11:23)

A man's heart deviseth his way: but the LORD directeth his steps. (Proverbs 16:9)

And the tongue is a fire, a world of iniquity: so is the tongue among our members, that it defileth the whole body, and setteth on fire the course of nature; and it is set on fire of hell. (James 3:6)

Whoso keepeth his mouth and his tongue keepeth his soul from troubles. (Proverbs 21:23)

I create the fruit of the lips; Peace, peace to him that is far off, and to him that is near, saith the LORD; and I will heal him. (Isaiah 57:19)

The mouth of a righteous man is a well of life: but violence covereth the mouth of the wicked. (Proverbs 10:11)

The words of the wicked are to lie in wait for blood: but the mouth of the upright shall deliver them. (Proverbs 12:6)

A man shall be satisfied with good by the fruit of his mouth: and the recompence of a man's hands shall be rendered unto him. (Proverbs 12:14)

There is that speaketh like the piercings of a sword: but the tongue of the wise is health. (Proverbs 12:18)

He that keepeth his mouth keepeth his life: but he that openeth wide his lips shall have destruction. (Proverbs 13:3)

> In the mouth of the foolish is a rod of pride:
> but the lips of the wise shall preserve them.
> (Proverbs 14:3)

> A wholesome tongue is a tree of life: but
> perverseness therein is a breach in the spirit.
> (Proverbs 15:4)

> The tongue of the wise useth knowledge
> aright: but the mouth of fools poureth out fool-
> ishness. (Proverbs 15:2)

> The heart of the wise teacheth his mouth,
> and addeth learning to his lips. (Proverbs 16:23)

> Pleasant words are as an honeycomb, sweet
> to the soul, and health to the bones. (Proverbs
> 16:24)

You can see from a few references that God's Word has a lot to say about the words we speak and their effect on you and your health.

God's Word will heal your body, but it does it through spiritual means. Healing can be received into the human spirit through the Word. Once it is conceived there, it permeates the physical body.

Just as you would take medicine into your physical body to aid healing by physical means, so you must receive God's Word concerning healing into your spirit for supernatural healing.

God's Word is perfect.

> The law of the Lord is perfect, converting
> the soul: the testimony of the Lord is sure, mak-
> ing wise the simple. (Psalm 19:7)

The law of the Lord is perfect. It is supernatural medicine. It works through the human spirit and is a spiritual cure, *but like any other medicine, it must be applied on a regular basis.*

You must speak God's Word to your individual circumstance or situation. The ball is in your court. God is listening to the words that you are speaking.

James 1:21 tells us, "To receive with meekness the engrafted word, which is able to save your soul." Once the Word of God is engrafted into your spirit, it produces results in the body as well.

Psalms 107: 20 tells us, "God sent His word and healed them." Notice that it didn't say that God sent his Word to heal, but He sent His word *and* healed. God considers it done.

God is no respecter of persons, but He does respect faith in His word.

Proverbs 4:20–22 tells us, "My son, attend to my words; incline thine ear unto my sayings. Let them not depart from thine eyes; keep them in the midst of thine heart. For they are life unto those that find them, and health to all their flesh."

First notice that God's Word is life to us. It is also health, or medicine, to all your flesh.

God's Word will heal your body, but it does it though spiritual means. Healing can be received into the human spirit by your words (based on the Word of God). Once it is conceived there, it permeates the physical body.

I can't say it enough: just as you would take medicine into your physical body to aid healing by physical means, you must receive God's Word concerning healing into your spirit for supernatural healing for your body.

When God's Word becomes engrafted or infused into your spirit, it has become a part of you. Then your flesh will reflect the life of that Word. When God's Word concerning healing takes root in your flesh, it becomes greater than the disease, and healing is the result.

When you speak God's Word from your heart, then faith gives substance to the promises of God. Your faith frames your world daily. Jesus made it plain in Matthew 12:35. "A good man out of the good treasure of his heart brings forth good things."

In the first chapter of Genesis, every time God spoke, creation took place. Words are the carriers of faith. Hebrews 11:3 tells us. "Through faith we understand that the worlds were framed by the word of God." Without words, there wouldn't have been any creation. Your words create images, and eventually, you will live out the reality of that image.

Every time you speak your faith, it creates a stronger image inside you. If it's healing you desire, the healing image is created by God's Word and your continual affirmation and agreement with it. Eventually, that image will be perfected by the Word of God, and you will begin to see yourself well.

A good example of this is found in Mark 5:25–28, where the woman with the issue of blood said, "If I may but touch his clothes, I shall be made whole." She continued to speak until she saw herself well.

This woman hoped to be healed as she pressed through the crowd. The Amplified Classic Bible says, "For she kept saying if I only touch His garments, I shall be restored to health." That hope was her goal. She didn't look healed. She didn't feel healed, but she began filling hope with faith-filled words: "I shall be restored to health. I shall be… I shall be…"

I am sure that her mind said, *When?* Not only that, I am sure that her mind said, *You don't look any better, so you're not any better.* She then began to answer human reasoning by being more specific. "When I touch His garment, I shall be made whole."

She set her own point of contact to receive her healing. Her words penetrated her spirit, and she began to see herself well. When she touched His clothes, her touch of faith made a demand on the covenant of God and the anointing that was upon Jesus.

What she was doing was allowing her faith to speak. When she acted out what she said and touched His garment, the faith that was in her became the substance of her hope, and her words became a living reality.

Faith gives substance to hope. Notice it was her faith that made a demand on the healing anointing that was upon Jesus. Faith gave substance to her hope, and healing was manifested in her body. Faith is the substance of things hoped for (Hebrews 11:1). Hope is important, but hope lacks substance until filled with faith. Hope is only a goal setter. Her hope was to be healed, but hope didn't heal her. Faith gave substance to her hope.

Her faith gave substance to and brought about the manifestation of healing that was already hers because of the covenant. But she had to believe it and receive it by faith. In her instance, it was to touch His clothes.

Psalm 107:2 says, "Let the redeemed of the Lord say so, whom He has redeemed for the hand of the enemy."

The words of Jesus said in Mark 9:23, "If thou canst believe, all things are possible to them that believe."

> And the Lord said, if ye had faith as a grain of mustard seed, ye might say unto this sycamine tree, Be thou plucked up by the root, and be thou planted in the sea; and it should obey you. (Luke 17:6)

> For verily I say unto you, That whosoever shall say unto this mountain, Be thou removed, and be thou cast into the sea; and shall not doubt in his heart, but shall believe that those things which he saith shall come to pass; he shall have whatsoever he saith.[24] Therefore I say unto you, what things soever ye desire, when ye pray, believe that ye receive them, and ye shall have them. (Mark 11:23–24)

Romans 4:17 tells us, "God calleth those things that be not as though they were." This is a great example of a Bible principle that we, as believers, should also practice.

God's word is medicine spoken to all our flesh (Proverbs 4:22). It's the most powerful medicine available today, and it is capable of healing your body without side effects.

Psalm 107:20 tells us that God sent His word and healed them.

Isaiah 53:5–6 and 1 Peter 2:24 let us know that healing is a fact as far as God is concerned.

Healing belongs to us because it was part of God's atonement through Jesus.

Let me say this again: I'm not teaching against doctors or medicine, but don't depend on that alone to keep you healthy. There are some diseases that medical science cannot cure. If you need a doctor, please go and see a doctor. Many lives are saved every year though medical help. There are medicines today that are beneficial in aiding the body's healing process.

If you are taking medicine, mix your faith with it, because there are some medicines with many side effects that seem to be worse than the disease. However, most medicines will help hold down the symptoms while you are applying God's principles concerning healing and health.

It is true that God has provided healing for us through His word, but we must learn to appropriate that healing by making the Word of God a part of our daily vocabulary. It takes time to renew your mind and develop faith in your words as well as God's Word.

Not only that, it takes time to develop your faith, so I don't advocate that you throw your medicine away and rely on confession alone unless the Lord directs you to do so. If you have a life-and-death situation where the doctor says if you don't have an operation immediately, you will die, my advice would be to have the operation and believe God, to use the doctors and for a speedy recovery. Use common sense, and don't do foolish things through spiritual pride and call it faith.

It takes time to operate in these principles. Operate on your level of faith, but don't stay on that level forever. Continue in God's Word until you develop faith in the healing power of God's Word. And don't let anyone put you under condemnation for going to the doctor.

Operating in these principles is not easy. It takes discipline and commitment. It's not just good enough to read these confessions occasionally. I encourage you to confess the Word of God over you and your body as many times a day with authority if necessary.

God declares that His word will not return to Him void.

Isaiah 55:11 tells us, "So shall my word be that goeth forth out of my mouth: it shall not return unto me void, but it shall accomplish that which I please, and it shall prosper in the thing whereto I sent it."

We are to return His word by giving voice to it, and He will create the fruit of our lips. Make it a practice to take God's medicine on a regular basis, just as you would any other medicine. Then it will be life to you and health to your flesh.

Romans 10:6, 8 says that "the righteousness which is of faith says…the word is nigh thee, even in thy mouth and in thy heart."

Notice the word is first in your mouth and then in your heart. God's Word becomes engrafted into your heart as you speak it. There is nothing more important to your faith than declaring what God has said about you with your own voice.

When you do this, some would say that you are denying what exists, but that's not true at all. You are establishing what God has said to be true concerning healing, even though it is not yet a reality in your body.

You don't deny that sickness exists, but you deny its right to exist in your body because you have been redeemed from the curse of the law and delivered from the authority of darkness (Galatians 3:13; Colossians 1:13).

When you are sick and confess that you are healed by the stripes of Jesus, you are speaking and agreeing with what God has already given you, even though it is not yet manifested. This is God's method of calling things that are not as though they were until they are.

There are some who have misunderstood this principle, and they call things that are as though they are not. In other words, they deny what exists. The power is in calling for healing and health by mixing faith with God's Word.

If you are sick, you don't deny that you are sick, but if you are always confessing sickness, you are establishing your present circumstance to yourself. Denying sickness won't make you well, but by mixing faith with God's Word, you are agreeing with the promises of God to be manifest in your body. This will cause you to be fully persuaded, and healing is the result.

There are some which would say that you are lying if you confess you are healed when you are sick. No, you are simply speaking and believing for healing that God has already provided.

What you are doing is practicing God's medicine. You are proclaiming what God has said in His Word to be truth, regardless of your present condition.

> Who his own self bare our sins in his own
> body on the tree, that we, being dead to sins,
> should live unto righteousness: by whose stripes
> ye were healed. (1 Peter 2:24)

Your body will listen to you, and it will obey you if you believe and not doubt in your heart. Your words have more effect on your body than anyone else's word. One mistake that so many Christians make is that they call things that are the way they are. By doing this, they are establishing the present condition or circumstance in their heart, mind, and also in their body.

> Let this mind be in you, which was also in
> Christ Jesus. (Philippians 2:5)

You have a God-given right to exercise authority over your body. How many times have you said things like "Every time I eat that, it makes me sick," "My back is killing me," "Those kids are driving me crazy," "This time of year, I always get the flu"?

Your own words are giving instruction to your body, and your immune system will eventually respond to your instruction.

Paul tells us in Romans 8:13, "For if we live after the flesh you shall die; but if you through the Spirit do mortify the deeds of the flesh, you shall live." Your flesh wants to say things like "This is just the way it is." However, if trained correctly by the Word of God, your spirit will say it the way God has said it in His Word.

Your body will respond to the demand of the human spirit. If you feed your spirit man God's Word, it will make demands on the flesh to line up with the Word of God.

There is more truth in Mark 11:23 than most people realize.

> For verily I say unto you, That whosoever
> shall say unto this mountain, Be thou removed,
> and be thou cast into the sea; and shall not doubt
> in his heart, but shall believe that those things
> which he saith shall come to pass; he shall have
> whatsoever he saith. (Mark 11:23)

You can have what you say in faith, but most people are saying what they have. If you put this into practice and make it a way of life, your body will respond to your faith demands that are based on the authority of God's holy Word.

God's Word is an incorruptible seed, and it produces after its kind.

No, it will not happen just because you say it, but saying it is involved in causing it to happen. Saying it is the way you plant the seed for what you need. The spoken Word of God imparts life into your physical body.

John 6:63 tells us, "It is the spirit that quickeneth; the flesh profiteth nothing: the words that I speak unto you, they are spirit, and they are life."

Faith doesn't speak to your present. Faith speaks to your future, and your future speaks to your present. The revelation is that Christ has put recovery in your future (Psalm 34:19; Jeremiah 30:19). This is the wisdom that can speak to your present so that faith can operate from a different viewpoint.

The apostle Paul instructs us to pray without ceasing (1 Thessalonians 5:16–18). We are a three part being of spirit, soul, and body. The body can be healed, the soul can be delivered, but the spirit needs to be aligned.

WOW (words of wisdom): If you align your spirit with God's Word, it will be like God. If you line it with other things, it will become like other things.

Always remember, *the ball is in your court*. You can *dribble*, *shoot*, or *pass*.

CHAPTER 8

It Is Finished

When Jesus said, "It is finished," none is more important than those words. Found only in the gospel of John, the Greek word for "it is finished" is *tetelestai,* an accounting term that means "paid in full."

Jesus's finished work on the cross was the beginning of new life for all who were once dead in trespasses and sins but who are now made alive with Christ (Ephesians 2:1,5). When Jesus had received the sour wine, he said, "It is finished," and He bowed His head and gave up His spirit (John 19:30).

When we think about the sacrifice that Jesus endured for us, and the unbearable physical pain that He endured, it's hard to comprehend. The Bible tells us how He was beaten nearly to the point of death with a whip that had metal tips on it.

- It tells us how a crown of thorns was driven into His scalp.
- It tells us how nails were punched through His hands and feet as He was being nailed to the cross that He was made to carry.
- It tells us how He was raised into the air to suffocate in one of the most inhumane and cruel forms of capital punishment ever known.

In the book of Isaiah 52:14 NLT, it tells us that "many were amazed when they saw Him beaten and blooded, so disfigured that one could scarcely know that He was a person."

We must understand that Jesus was in the flesh, just like us. In the book of Philippians 2:6–8 NLT, it tells us:

> Though He was God, He did not demand
> and cling to the rights of God. He made Himself
> nothing. He took the humble position of a slave
> and appeared in human form. And in human
> form, He obediently humbled Himself even fur-
> ther by dying a criminal's death on the cross.

I thank God for His mercy that we are not consumed. Because of His compassion failing not, they are new to us every morning (Lamentations 3:22, 23). The same way God gives us a choice to choose the decisions we make in this life, Jesus had a choice to make concerning His death. In the book of Matthew 26:39, it tells us "And He went a little further and fell on His face, and prayed saying, 'Father, if it be possible, let this cup pass from me: nevertheless not as I will, but as thou will.'"

I believe that Jesus thought about us, and He knew that the choice He made would be a permanent decision. Matthew 26:53 tells us, "Thinkest thou that I cannot now pray to my Father, and He shall presently give me more than twelve legions of angels." Jesus could have prayed, and His Father would have sent more than twelve legions of angels down to rescue and protect Him (one legion is six thousand angels. Twelve legions is seventy-two thousand angels).

My friends, it's hard not to focus on the pain that Jesus endured for us. Because of the price that was paid for us, we have a way to get back in right standing with Him. The first Adam lost everything, but God made a way for us through Jesus, that we can have a right to the tree of life.

But I want us to look at another way I believe Jesus was made to suffer in the moments before His crucifixion. I want us to consider the emotional pain that I believe Jesus endured as those who were closest to Him turned their backs on Him.

Jesus personally chose twelve disciples whom He poured Himself into. They were what we may refer to as Jesus's family. Jesus loved these men and deposited Himself into them, yet He knew before they did that a couple of them would publicly betray Him.

I have learned that although you can know something in your heart, when it manifests or when it happens, it can have an effect on you emotionally.

I have learned since I've been on this journey called life—and I'm sure some of you have learned this too—that emotional pain can sometimes be as painful as physical pain (if you haven't learned that yet, just keep on living).

I have experienced, and I know people who have personally poured their life into their children, husband, wife, and family, and have experienced betrayal from some of them.

The one that comes to my mind first that turned his back on Jesus is Judas. It was Judas's betrayal that led to the crucifixion. In the book of Luke 22:3, it tells us that Satan entered into Judas. In the book of John 13:2, it tells us that the devil put into Judas's heart to betray Jesus.

Judas went to the chief priest and officers and told them how he could betray Jesus into their hands when there wouldn't be a crowd of people around Him. They bribed him with thirty pieces of silver worth $324.60.

(Have you ever heard the old saying that money talks?)

How it must have broken Jesus's heart when Judas stepped out of the crowd of those who came to arrest Him and betrayed Him with a kiss on the cheek. WOW (words of wisdom): Not everybody that hugs you loves you, and not everybody that smiles in your face is your friend.

Another one of Jesus's disciples that turned their back on Him was Peter. Peter was one of Jesus's closest friends who He chose to be a witness to key moments in His earthy ministry.

Peter was there for Jesus's transfiguration on the mountain and at Gethsemane on the eve of His sacrifice. It tells us that as Jesus was being beaten and ridiculed, Peter was distancing himself.

When Jesus told His disciples that they were going to desert Him, Peter was the one who said, "Lord, not me. If everyone else deserts you, it won't be me."

Jesus told Peter, "Peter, before the rooster crows, you will deny me three times."

In the book of Mark 14, it tells us that Peter was approached three times and was asked if he was associated with Jesus, and three times, Peter denied Jesus, even going so far as to swear, "I don't even know this man whom you speak of."

At the time when Jesus was being accused and beaten, His friends turned their backs on Him. What emotional pain this must have caused even as Jesus knew it was coming.

I have experienced that people will talk tough and tell you they will be there for you if you need them—when things are going good. But I have also learned that when things get tough, the tough get going.

I thank God for using people, because the only God so many people will ever see is the God that is in us, that we represent. I believe that everyone knows what a Christian or a child of God shouldn't do, but people are searching for those that are true examples of the true and living God.

Although God can supernaturally meet your every need, He also uses people to get His work done and be an extension of His hand. Although He can use other avenues, He doesn't want us to look to man to supply our needs; He (God) wants us to have our faith and our trust in Him and in the finished work of the cross.

Getting back to Judas; When Judas came to his senses, and saw that his plan didn't work the way he thought and that Pilate had condemned Jesus to die, it says that Judas was filled with remorse (Matthew 27:3 NLT) because he knew that he was the one who had betrayed Jesus.

WOW (words of wisdom): be careful how you treat people and be careful how you live your life, because sometimes you can get there, but you can't get back. Judas tried to go back and fix what he had messed up. He went back to the temple, where the leading priest and the others were with the thirty pieces of silver. He said, "Look, I have sinned, and I have betrayed an innocent man."

They looked at him and said, "What is that to us? That's your problem."

The story tells us that when Judas saw that they wouldn't take the money back, he threw it on the floor, and he went out and hung himself. You see, Judas went there, but he couldn't get back. He wasn't able to make his wrong right.

The question we need to ask ourselves is this: What am I missing by turning my back on Jesus? You might be saying that you are not turning your back on Jesus.

If you have not accepted Jesus as your Savior, so that when this life is over on earth, you will live with Him in Heaven, you are turning your back on Him and the price that He paid for you.

You are free not to accept Jesus as your Savior; God gives us all a free will. However, you are not free from the consequences of your choice. If you choose not to accept Jesus as your Savior and you die, you will go to hell.

(I know that's tight, but it's right.)

Judas missed out on that choice; he went out and hung himself. But salvation is available to all of us today. Jesus just didn't get up from the grave: He got up with all power in His hand. Revelation 1:18 NLT tells us, "I am he that liveth, and was dead; and behold, I am alive for evermore, A-men; and have the keys of hell, and of death."

When Jesus took those thirty-nine stripes, and when He said, "It is finished," it was finished! Everybody that accepts Jesus as their Savior, He comes and lives on the inside of them. Romans 8:11 tells us, "But if the same spirit of him that raised up Jesus from the dead dwell in you, he that raised up Christ from the dead shall also quicken your mortal body by His spirit that dwelleth in you."

Not only does He come and live on the inside of us when we accept Him as our Savior but He deposits His resurrection power on the inside of us (Acts 1:8; Luke 9:1; Luke 10:19; Matthew 18:18; 1John 4:4).

When Jesus looked down from that old rugged cross at those who had mocked, spit on, slapped, and beat Him, at those who had jammed that crown of thorns deep into His forehead, nailed Him to the cross, and turned their backs on Him, He still cried out, "Father, forgive them, for they know not what they do."

The Lord instructed me to write this book to encourage you to learn who Jesus really is. To let somebody know that you don't have to continue to turn your back on Him. He wants everyone to make it right with Him while they still have blood running warm in their body.

Not your mother, your father, your husband, your wife, your sister, or your brother. He wants everyone to make it right with Him. You don't have to miss out on what has been made available for you at the cross.

If you have not made it right with God, the good news is this: you still have breath in your body, and God is giving you another chance to make it right with Him. If you have not accepted Jesus as your Savior, you shouldn't turn your back on God another day for all that He has done for you and not accept the free gift of eternal life that He paid for you to have.

Every one of us is going out into eternity one day. Today could be our last day. There are many people that may know of Jesus and what He has accomplished on the cross; however, they won't make a decision about Him as their Savior.

But let me tell you this. Indecision is a decision; making no decision for Jesus is making a decision about Jesus.

Jesus's forgiveness and the finished work of the cross is just as good and just as powerful today as it was over two thousand years ago. The power of the Holy Spirit can still change your world if you let Him.

Committing sins is not what sends a person to hell. If that were the case, we would all go to hell because it tells us in Romans 3:10, "As it is written, there is none righteous, no not one."

> For all have sinned and come short of the
> glory of God. (Romans 3:23)

You sin because you are a sinner, born in sin (Psalm 51:5). Jesus will clean you of your sins if you let Him. The only reason that a person will go to hell is if they don't accept Jesus as their Savior while the blood is still running warm in their veins.

Death is certain for all of us. But when death comes is uncertain.

Hebrews 9:27 tells us, "And as it is appointed unto man once to die, but after this the judgment."

You should want to be certain that when death do comes, you will go and be with the Lord in heaven.

If you have not made it right with God by accepting Him as your Savior and you want to be certain that when death comes, God will welcome you into His kingdom, I want to say a prayer with you. You might not understand it now, but with your hope in the resurrected Jesus, one day you will understand that this was the best decision you made in this life.

If you want to be certain that when this life is over, Jesus will welcome you into His kingdom, say this prayer, and mean it from your heart:

Dear God, I know that I was born in sin, and I can't save myself. But you said in the book of Romans 10:9, if I confess with my mouth that Jesus is Lord and believe in my heart that God raised Him from the dead, I shall be saved.

I open the door of my heart on today, and I invite you to come into my life. Forgive me of all of my sins. Fill me with your spirit. I give you permission to do a work in me so that I can live a life that is pleasing to you. I accept you now as my Lord and my Savior. I now look forward to you welcoming me into your kingdom in heaven when this life is over on earth.

In Jesus's name, amen.

If you said that prayer, you are now a child of God, and your name just got written in the Lamb's book of life. The real you (your spirit) is now a new creation. Second letter to the Corinthians 5:17

tells us, "Therefore if any man be in Christ, he is a new creature: old things are passed away; Behold, all things are become new."

You must understand this: although the real you (your spirit) is now a new creature, your mind and your body are still the same. Now it's time to grow spiritually so that you can live a victorious life.

We at Blessed to Be a Blessing Outreach Ministries (BTBAB) would like to send you a little booklet titled *Your New Life in Christ: Things You Need to Know in Order to Grow Spiritually.*

You can contact us at BTBAB.NET. Visit the Contact page and leave us your name and mailing address, and we will be more than happy to send you this free booklet.

ABOUT THE AUTHOR

Dr. Joseph Morrison is founder/CEO of Blessed to Be a Blessing Outreach Ministries Inc., a 501(c)(3) nonprofit ministry. He is married to Mennie Morrison who serves as the administrator of the ministry. Currently, they have six children, twelve grandchildren, and one godchild. Dr. Morrison resides in York, South Carolina. He is currently serving as senior pastor of The Center Fellowship in Fort Mill, South Carolina.

The ministry of BTBAB is a local outreach ministry located in York, South Carolina, but recognized in both the Carolinas and serves even beyond. The ministry's focus is evangelism and assisting the underprivileged. Dr. Morrison has served in full-time pastoral ministry to seniors at a local assisted living center and is currently serving part-time. He has had other ministry service with several local churches in the area, with over six years of service with one of those churches.

Dr. Morrison is a retired veteran of the United States Army. He has had the privilege of working as a chaplain for a local arena football team. Currently he is serving with the Billy Graham Rapid Response Team as a chaplain with CICM, Strategic Ministry, and FEMA training since 2007. Dr. Morrison has earned his doctorate degree in ministry with a concentration on biblical teaching and leadership from Ames Christian University, Fort Myers, Florida.

The work that God has chosen him to do extends beyond the four walls of the church. Ministry travels consist of not only the preaching of the gospel to local churches but also ministering to the needs of those that are less fortunate around the world. Dr. Morrison's service as a chaplain with the Billy Graham Rapid Response Team has afforded him the great opportunity to deploy to many areas across the country, helping those that have been affected by various forms of disaster and devastation, providing emotional and spiritual care. His heart and love for his Lord Jesus Christ is evident in all that he does because he serves God and others with a true servant's heart!